An Illustrated History of
CARLISLE'S RAILWAYS

By
W A C Smith
Paul Anderson

The light fades. On 5th August 1967 Jubilee No. 45562 ALBERTA rolls into Citadel half an hour late with the 06.40 from Birmingham New Street to Glasgow Central. The train went forward over the Glasgow & South Western route behind a Britannia Pacific. Photograph W.A.C. Smith.

Copyright Irwell Press
ISBN 1-871608-73-2

Front cover top. Until the overall roof was shortened during the late 1950s, the south end of Carlisle Citadel provided a spectacular setting for photographers. Furthermore, most through expresses changed engines at the station, thus adding to the interest. In early afternoon sunshine, on 1st September 1954, Coronation No.46253 CITY OF ST ALBANS, is ready to take over the 9.00am Perth - Euston while class 5 4-6-0 No.45306 waits for the 10.40am Glasgow - Liverpool. 'Crab' 2-6-0 No.42881 stands in the former Midland bay with empty stock. Photograph W.A.C. Smith.

Front cover bottom. On 18th September 1956 passengers wave their final farewells as the up 'Royal Scot' leaves Carlisle with Camden Pacific No.46229 DUCHESS OF HAMILTON very much in charge. The very attractive non-standard tartan headboard added a distinctive touch to the flagship of West Coast expresses. Forty years on, DUCHESS OF HAMILTON was still making the occasional appearance at Carlisle, in its much-deserved preserved role. Photograph F.W. Shuttleworth.

Back cover. Ex-North British class N15 0-6-2T No.69155 at Dentonholme yard with trip 48 on 19th September 1959, its lengthy mixed train including at least five new parcels vans. A great deal of engineering work was necessary to build the former G&SW depot on the slopes of the River Caldew, as is apparent in this view. Photograph G.M. Staddon, Neville Stead Collection.

Coronation Pacific No.46252 CITY OF LEICESTER makes light work of the climb to Beattock summit as it passes Harthope unbanked with the 9.25am Crewe - Aberdeen on 29th July 1961. This was the end of the Glasgow Fair holiday and eight specials had to be slotted in between the fifteen timetabled services. Photograph W.A.C. Smith.

First Published in the United Kingdom by
IRWELL PRESS 1997
59A, High Street, Clophill, Bedfordshire MK45 4BE
Printed in Huddersfield by The Amadeus Press

CONTENTS

Chapter One
The Great Railway City 1

Chapter Two
North Eastern 7

Chapter Three
Maryport & Carlisle 15

Chapter Four
London & North Western 23

Chapter Five
Caledonian 29

Chapter Six
Glasgow & South Western 37

Chapter Seven
North British 43

Chapter Eight
Midland 49

Chapter Nine
Citadel 55

Chapter Ten
Goods Traffic 69

Chapter Eleven
Engine Sheds 81

Chapter Twelve
Citadel 150 87

ACKNOWLEDGEMENTS

The authors are indebted to the following people who provided invaluable help during the preparation of this book: Allison Gilliver of Coalville for typesetting the maps; Richard Casserley of Berkhamsted for his father's photographs of West Cumberland trains; Chris Hawkins of Clophill for additional material on the engine sheds; Robert Leslie of Carlisle for his views of the Maryport & Carlisle line; Tim Shuttleworth of Ludlow for processing W.A.C. Smith's negatives; Alan Thompson of Penshaw for J.W. Armstrong's Newcastle & Carlisle photographs; Juliet Whitworth of Barrow upon Soar for the line drawings. W.A.C. Smith wishes to thank Doris for her help, encouragement, patience and painstaking proof reading in Glasgow and this is echoed by Paul Anderson in Leicester.

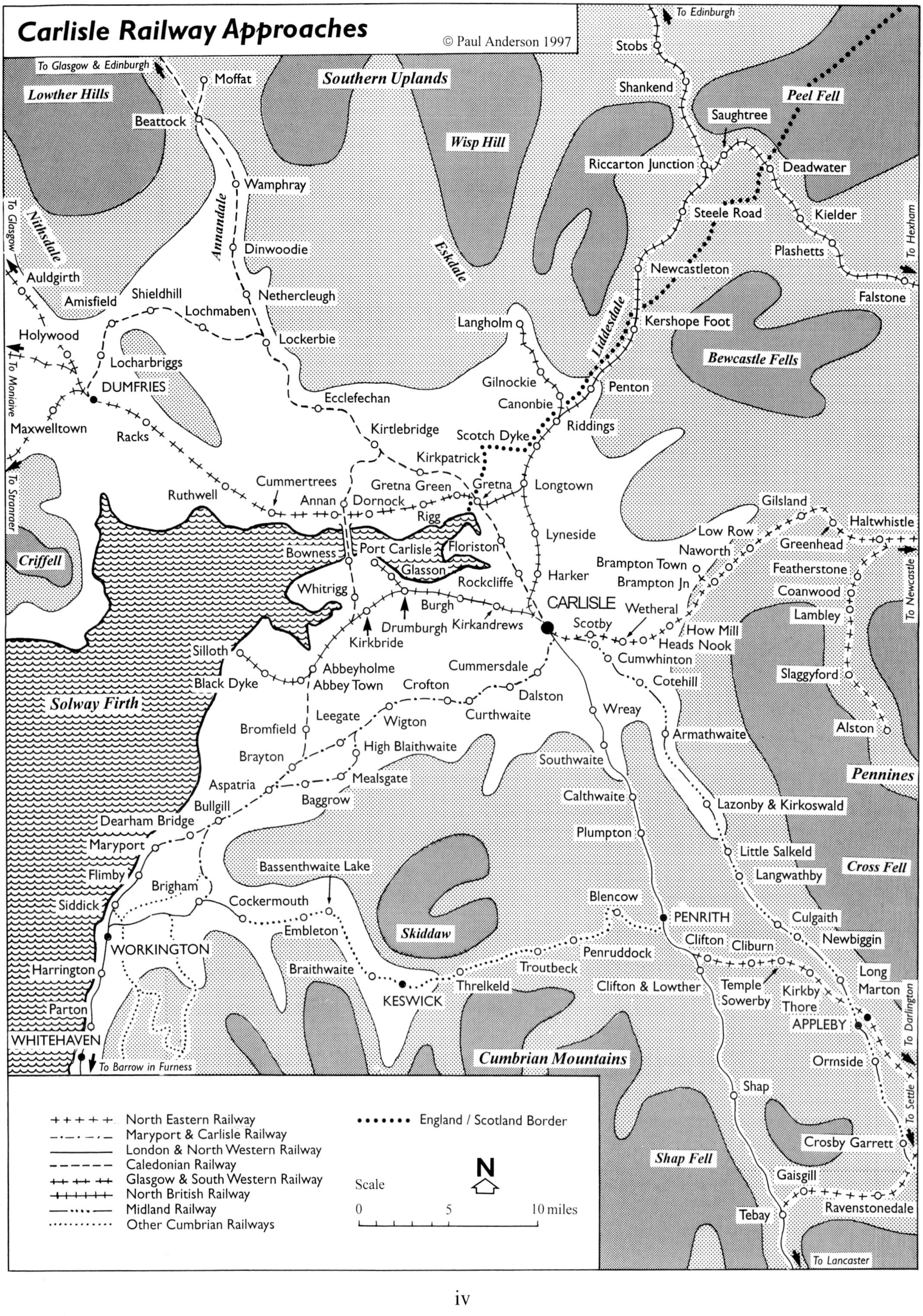

Carlisle Railway Approaches
© Paul Anderson 1997
To Glasgow & Edinburgh
To Edinburgh
Lowther Hills
Southern Uplands
Wisp Hill
Peel Fell
Moffat
Beattock
Stobs
Shankend
Saughtree
Riccarton Junction
Deadwater
Wamphray
Steele Road
Kielder
To Glasgow
Nithsdale
Annandale
Eskdale
Plashetts
To Hexham
Dinwoodie
Newcastleton
Falstone
Auldgirth
Amisfield
Shieldhill
Nethercleugh
Lochmaben
Liddesdale
Kershope Foot
Holywood
Lockerbie
Langholm
Bewcastle Fells
To Moniaive
Locharbriggs
DUMFRIES
Gilnockie
Penton
Ecclefechan
Canonbie
Maxwelltown
Racks
Kirtlebridge
Scotch Dyke
Riddings
Kirkpatrick
To Stranraer
Ruthwell
Cummertrees
Gretna Green
Gretna
Longtown
Annan
Dornock
Gilsland
Rigg
Haltwhistle
Lyneside
Low Row
Greenhead
Criffell
Bowness
Port Carlisle
Floriston
Naworth
Glasson
Brampton Town
Featherstone
Harker
To Newcastle
Rockcliffe
Brampton Jn
Coanwood
Whitrigg
CARLISLE
Wetheral
Lambley
Burgh
Drumburgh
Kirkandrews
Scotby
How Mill
Kirkbride
Heads Nook
Silloth
Cumwhinton
Abbeyholme
Cummersdale
Cotehill
Slaggyford
Black Dyke
Abbey Town
Crofton
Solway Firth
Dalston
Leegate
Wreay
Wigton
Curthwaite
Bromfield
Alston
Armathwaite
High Blaithwaite
Southwaite
Brayton
Pennines
Aspatria
Mealsgate
Calthwaite
Lazonby & Kirkoswald
Baggrow
Bullgill
Dearham Bridge
Plumpton
Little Salkeld
Maryport
Bassenthwaite Lake
Cross Fell
Flimby
Langwathby
Brigham
Blencow
Siddick
Cockermouth
PENRITH
Culgaith
Embleton
Skiddaw
WORKINGTON
Clifton
Cliburn
Newbiggin
Penruddock
Braithwaite
Troutbeck
Harrington
Temple Sowerby
Long Marton
Threlkeld
Clifton & Lowther
Kirkby Thore
KESWICK
To Darlington
Parton
APPLEBY
WHITEHAVEN
Cumbrian Mountains
To Barrow in Furness
Ormside
To Settle
Shap
Crosby Garrett
Shap Fell
Gaisgill
Ravenstonedale
Tebay
To Lancaster
North Eastern Railway
Maryport & Carlisle Railway
London & North Western Railway
Caledonian Railway
Glasgow & South Western Railway
North British Railway
Midland Railway
Other Cumbrian Railways
England / Scotland Border
N
Scale
0
5
10 miles

Chapter 1
THE GREAT RAILWAY CITY

In the text and illustrations which follow, well over fifty different classes of steam locomotives are seen to have frequented Carlisle during the period from the creation of British Railways in 1948 to the complete take-over by diesels in 1967. Up to a dozen other types at the end of their working lives appeared in the late 1940s and early 1950s but are not recorded here. When the huge range of engines owned by the seven independent companies serving Carlisle prior to 1923 is taken into account, it becomes clear that this was rather a special place. In fact no other railway centre in the world with just one main passenger station has experienced such a variety of motive power and, for that matter, train services. Furthermore, this accolade belongs to a city of modest size - even today its population is less than 100,000.

The explanation is a complex one involving a unique geographical setting, almost two thousand years of history and ruthless 19th century enterprise. With hindsight, it was almost inevitable that the Border City would play a crucial role in the Victorian railway revolution.

Carlisle stands at the confluence of the Eden and Caldew, just inland from the head of the Solway Firth. It is surrounded by the fertile red clay lowlands of the Solway Plain, but within twenty miles of the city high ground closes in on three sides. To the north, the Southern Uplands of Scotland present a mighty barrier of ancient slate stretching all the way from Stranraer to Berwickshire. To the east, Carboniferous limestone and Millstone Grit form the Pennines, the backbone of England. Rearing up to the south are the Cumbrian mountains, a mass of slate and volcanic rock forming that most beautiful of areas, the Lake District.

Although a number of rivers drain into the Solway, their valleys only penetrate so far into the uplands. Any route to Scotland or other parts of England had to seek out low points in the hills, and this particularly applied to the railways. North of the Border, Nithsdale led to the moorland gap between Sanquhar and the Ayr basin, there was a way out of Annandale to the Clyde valley via the lofty pass at Beattock, and at Whitrope it was possible to get through to the Tweed lowlands from Liddesdale.

To the east, the River Irthling led to the Tyne Gap at Gilsland, giving access to Newcastle. The path to the south was less easy. The Lake District mountains were a formidable obstacle and the way round the Cumbrian coast is circuitous. The Eden Valley looked promising, but high ground separated its headwaters from the Ribble Valley. Similarly, access to the Lune Gorge meant tackling the lofty moorland at Shap. The combined effect of the indented Solway Firth and the convergence of these various routes meant that Carlisle was bound to be a major communications centre for the north of England.

A number of major inlets from the Firth of Clyde in the north to the Bristol Channel in the south give the west coast of Britain its distinctive profile. As trade with America developed, three of these

Roaring safety valves and billowing smoke at the south end of Citadel on the damp Saturday afternoon of 13th August 1966, typifying the last days of steam. Britannia Pacific No.70010 OWEN GLENDOWER gets on the move from platform 3 with the 09.10 Dundee - Blackpool, which had come in via the Waverley route behind D1987. On the right, Black 5 No.45105 stands at platform 4 with the 11.05 from Glasgow to Blackpool, which had travelled via Dumfries. No.45312 waits in the centre road to take over the 11.35 relief from Glasgow to Manchester via Carstairs. Photograph W.A.C. Smith.

An Illustrated History of Carlisle's Railways

Although seven companies worked into Citadel prior to the Grouping of 1923, the London & North Western regarded itself as the senior partner; it was the 'Premier Line' after all. Claughton 4-6-0 No.2416 storms away from Carlisle with the 12.18pm express for Euston one sunny day in the early 1920s. Photograph J.F. Ward Collection.

gave rise to great industrial ports, namely Glasgow, Liverpool and Bristol. The Solway Firth did not develop in the same way, but the town of Carlisle assumed an importance much earlier than places which eventually outgrew it. The story began nearly two millennia ago.

During the winter of AD 72-73, the Romans marched north from their newly established base at York, crossed the Pennines at Stainmore and followed the River Eden to the sea. In the Solway lowlands they discovered early farmers who had cleared woodland to rear cattle, sheep and pigs. Under the leadership of Petillius Cerialis a fort was built and Carlisle was born. There were hostile tribes to the north, so in AD 122 Hadrian had a wall built from the Solway to the Tyne, to formalise the northern limit of his empire. Carlisle then became a frontier settlement, a role which it has performed ever since - even during the railway age.

Although the Roman fort was abandoned in AD 340, the village itself survived, only to be sacked by the Vikings in AD 876. By then, Cumbria was of great strategic importance to the Scottish and English kings alike and the settlement at the head of the Solway Firth was a focal point. By the Norman conquest, Carlisle was virtually a town - at a time when there were none in Scotland and few in England. King William II, son of William the Conqueror, built a timber castle in 1092 to repel the Scots and this was rebuilt as a stone fortress in the mid-1100s. At the same time the city walls were erected and an Augustinian priory established, the latter eventually forming the basis of the present cathedral.

During the 1200s, Carlisle prospered as the economic, social, fiscal, judicial and religious focus of Cumbria. There was a royal mint using silver from Alston and commodities passing through the town ranged from Egremont iron and sea coal from Whitehaven to squirrel skins, out of local woods. The Scottish border was defined in 1237, although this made no difference to the flourishing trade with communities in the Southern Uplands, in which wool was particularly important. Nevertheless, traumatic times lay ahead. In 1296 the Anglo-Scottish wars began and Carlisle's population swelled as the army of King Edward I moved in. The 1300s proved disastrous for the Border City - there were two devastating fires, the Black Death struck, and the Scots raided on no less than twenty occasions.

Peace came for a while, but a full scale war broke out between England and Scotland in 1456 and Carlisle was in the firing line yet again. A century later, the castle was strengthened when France and Scotland turned on England. In 1640 there was another threat from the Scots and the castle was refurbished, ready for siege. The Jacobite revolts of 1715 and 1745 gave rise to further anguish, but fortunately did not trouble the town. At long last the castle could languish in picturesque decay.

In the mid-1700s, Carlisle was a sleepy country town with a population of about 4,000 but the following hundred years saw a remarkable transformation. General Wade's Military Road from Newcastle, laid down during 1745 in response to the Jacobite rebellion, encouraged immigration and trade from the continent. Linen weavers arrived and by 1750 there were several water-powered mills on the River Caldew. Cotton spinning began in the 1790s and even larger mills began to dominate the western side of the town. During the early 1800s a number of foundries were established, supplying ironwork principally for the textile industry and agriculture. The Carlisle Canal opened in 1823, giving the Border City an outlet to the sea, and by 1831 Carlisle's population had reached 20,000.

By then, the Railway Age beckoned and the western section of the pioneering Newcastle & Carlisle line from Greenhead to London Road opened in 1836. Dixon's enormous seven-storey cotton mill in Shaddongate, the largest in England at the time, was completed during the same year. Through trains from Carlisle to Tyneside commenced in 1838. Meanwhile, the West Coast route from London to Scotland began to take shape, with Euston - Lancaster services starting in 1840 and much talk of an extension northwards. After a prolonged gestation, the Maryport & Carlisle Railway opened throughout in 1845 and the adventurous Lancaster & Carlisle line over bleak Shap Fell came into operation during 1846. Citadel station began its long career in September 1847 and through trains from Glasgow to

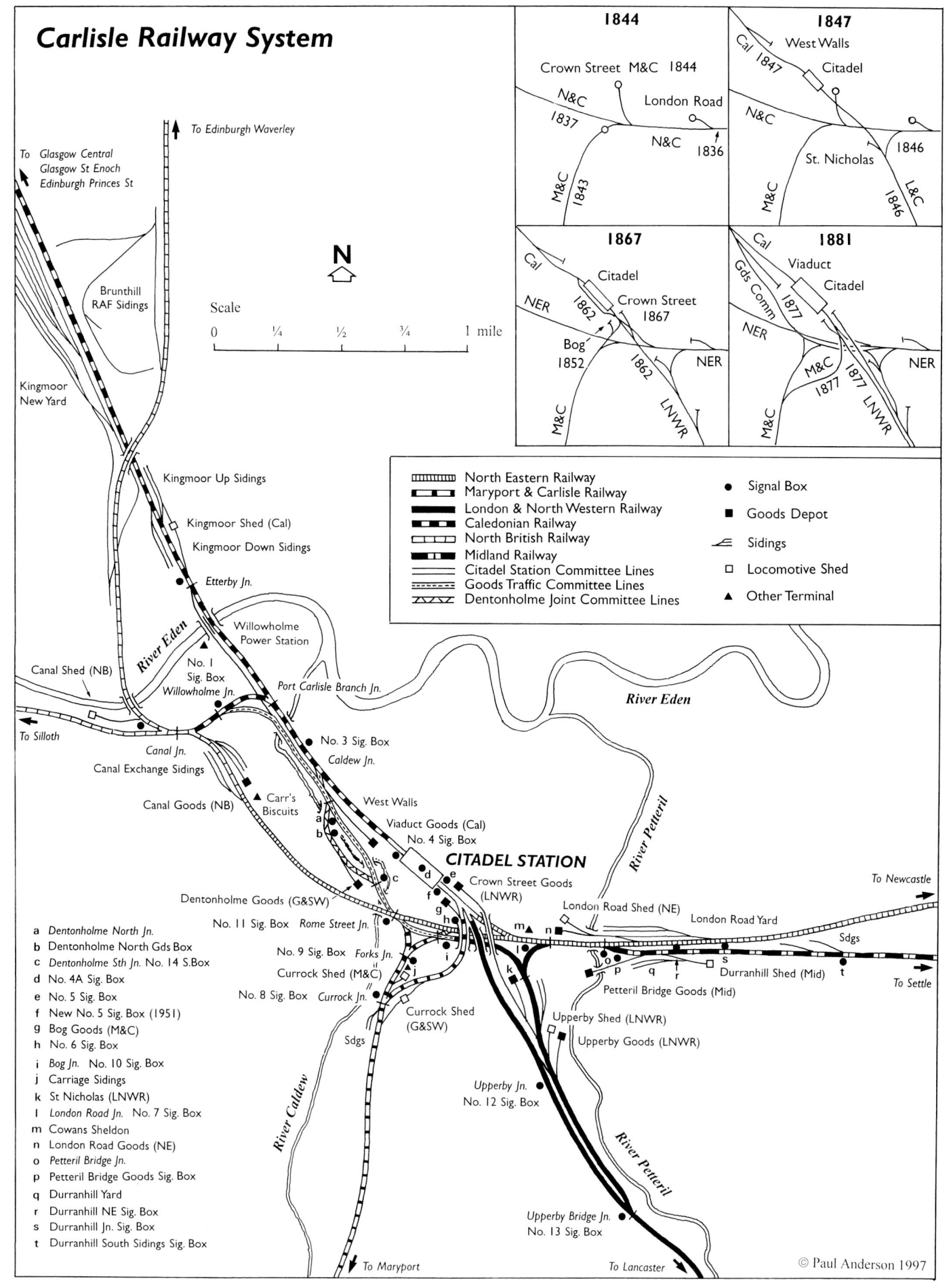

Carlisle Railway System

1844
Crown Street M&C 1844
N&C 1837
London Road
N&C 1836
M&C 1843

1847
Cal 1847
West Walls
Citadel
N&C
St. Nicholas 1846
M&C
L&C 1846

1867
Cal
Citadel 1862
Crown Street 1867
Bog 1852
NER
M&C 1862
LNWR

1881
Cal
Gds Comm 1877
Viaduct
Citadel
NER
M&C 1877
LNWR 1877

To Glasgow Central
Glasgow St Enoch
Edinburgh Princes St

To Edinburgh Waverley

Brunthill RAF Sidings

Kingmoor New Yard

Kingmoor Up Sidings

Kingmoor Shed (Cal)

Kingmoor Down Sidings

Etterby Jn.

River Eden

Willowholme Power Station

Canal Shed (NB)

No. 1 Sig. Box
Willowholme Jn.

Port Carlisle Branch Jn.

River Eden

To Silloth

Canal Jn.
Canal Exchange Sidings

No. 3 Sig. Box
Caldew Jn.

Canal Goods (NB)

Carr's Biscuits

West Walls
Viaduct Goods (Cal)
No. 4 Sig. Box

CITADEL STATION

River Petteril

To Newcastle

Crown Street Goods (LNWR)
London Road Shed (NE)
London Road Yard

Dentonholme Goods (G&SW)

No. 11 Sig. Box Rome Street Jn.

No. 9 Sig. Box Forks Jn.

Currock Shed (M&C)

No. 8 Sig. Box Currock Jn.

Currock Shed (G&SW)

Sdgs

Durranhill Shed (Mid)
Petteril Bridge Goods (Mid)

To Settle

Upperby Shed (LNWR)
Upperby Goods (LNWR)

River Caldew

Upperby Jn.
No. 12 Sig. Box

River Petteril

Upperby Bridge Jn.
No. 13 Sig. Box

To Maryport

To Lancaster

Legend:
- North Eastern Railway
- Maryport & Carlisle Railway
- London & North Western Railway
- Caledonian Railway
- North British Railway
- Midland Railway
- Citadel Station Committee Lines
- Goods Traffic Committee Lines
- Dentonholme Joint Committee Lines
- ● Signal Box
- ■ Goods Depot
- Sidings
- □ Locomotive Shed
- ▲ Other Terminal

a Dentonholme North Jn.
b Dentonholme North Gds Box
c Dentonholme Sth Jn. No. 14 S.Box
d No. 4A Sig. Box
e No. 5 Sig. Box
f New No. 5 Sig. Box (1951)
g Bog Goods (M&C)
h No. 6 Sig. Box
i Bog Jn. No. 10 Sig. Box
j Carriage Sidings
k St Nicholas (LNWR)
l London Road Jn. No. 7 Sig. Box
m Cowans Sheldon
n London Road Goods (NE)
o Petteril Bridge Jn.
p Petteril Bridge Goods Sig. Box
q Durranhill Yard
r Durranhill NE Sig. Box
s Durranhill Jn. Sig. Box
t Durranhill South Sidings Sig. Box

© Paul Anderson 1997

An Illustrated History of Carlisle's Railways

As trains became heavier, the LMS introduced new Pacifics on West Coast main line services through Carlisle. Stanier Princess 4-6-2s were regularly employed until the Coronation streamliners took over. On 21st June 1937, No.6207 PRINCESS ARTHUR OF CONNAUGHT storms past Upperby yard with the Glasgow - Euston 'Royal Scot' comprising thirteen coaches. Photograph H.C. Casserley.

London via the new Caledonian main line commenced in 1848.

These early railways immediately stimulated industry in Carlisle. Clockmakers, already established by the 1830s, found numerous outlets for their products as scores of new stations opened, while foundries began to supply all manner of components, from wagon wheels to pointwork. Cowans Sheldon was formed in 1846 to build dockyard and railway breakdown cranes. The two partners hailed from the North East and were associated with the Newcastle & Carlisle, Sheldon reputedly having driven one of the first trains. In 1831 J.D. Carr started making biscuits in the Border City. During 1849 he installed the first biscuit-cutting machine and capitalised on his technological lead by using railways to establish a national, then international, trade.

By 1850 Carlisle was a dirty, overcrowded industrial town with 35,000 inhabitants. Crime was rife and cholera epidemics frequent. Water from the numerous wells was unfit for drinking, sanitation did not exist, and up to twenty people lived in one room at certain lodging houses. Vile privvies and 'dunghills' were a feature of such establishments. Although the railways were partially responsible for the growth of such appalling housing, they also displaced a fair amount of property, notably some of the early industrial sites.

Competition between different railway companies, a feature of Carlisle for over seventy years, effectively began in 1850 when the Glasgow & South Western was formed. This new concern inherited the Gretna - Dumfries line, opened during 1848, and gained admission to Citadel in 1851. The Port Carlisle canal was converted into a railway during 1854 and an extension to Silloth followed two years later. Meanwhile, Carlisle itself continued to expand. Until 1853 the city had been somewhat hemmed in by its ancient walls and the River Caldew, but from then on the new Nelson Bridge allowed Dentonholme to mushroom. The powerful London & North Western Railway began to influence affairs at Citadel when it leased the Lancaster & Carlisle in 1859. Shortly afterwards the station was extended to cope with additional passenger trains - North British workings via the Waverley route commenced in 1862 and Newcastle & Carlisle services were transferred from London Road in 1863. Industry was evolving as well. By 1870 cotton manufacturing was beginning to decline, but Hudson Scott, formed the previous year to make biscuit tins, was destined to become a founder member of the huge Metal Box conglomerate. Tyler & Co., which supplied signalling equipment for railways throughout the world for over fifty years, was established in 1873.

There was a major development at Citadel in 1876 when Midland passenger trains began to run over the Settle & Carlisle line. In partnership with this new English ally, the G&SW and North British became part of an Anglo-Scottish operation rivalling the established and somewhat haughty Caledonian/LNWR West Coast alliance. Fortunately, there was a degree of co-operation as well - the goods avoiding lines, opened in 1877, were a joint venture by the LNWR, Caledonian, G&SW and Midland. Between 1878 and 1881, Citadel was rebuilt again, this time on a massive scale. Rather less dramatic but nevertheless a familiar backdrop to views of the north end of the station for well over a century, the *Viaduct Hotel* opened in the late 1870s, for commercial travellers arriving by train.

A new goods depot and associated loop at Dentonholme were opened by the Midland, G&SW and North British in 1883, but following this development,

A busy scene at Citadel in 1919. Glasgow & South Western Drummond 4-4-0 No.327 in immaculate condition stands on the left and a LNW Claughton waits on the other centre road with empty stock. A Midland express with a Compound in charge has just arrived at the down main platform. Photograph H. Gordon Tidey, courtesy R.M. Casserley.

An Illustrated History of Carlisle's Railways

Class A2/3 Pacific No.60522 STRAIGHT DEAL at Citadel on 12th July 1964 prior to taking over the twelve coach Sunday afternoon down working from Liverpool and Manchester. Despite leaving Carlisle 41 minutes late, the Polmadie engine had cut back 22 minutes of the deficit on arrival at Glasgow Central. Photograph W.A.C. Smith.

Carlisle's railway network saw no major investment for nearly seventy years. The city itself, still quite compact and lacking suburban stations, did however gain a 3ft 6in gauge electric tramway in 1900. This extended to Boundary Road, Petteril Bridge and Dentonholme, a total of 5½ route miles, and was worked by twelve cars. It was purchased by the Ribble bus company in 1930 and closed the following year.

Another Carlisle institution enjoyed a rather longer existence. During World War I the largest armaments factory in Europe was established near Longtown and by 1916 no less than 5,000 men and women regularly descended on the city's public houses, adding to the 'frontier town' feeling in no small way! Munitions production was seriously undermined, so the government decided to act. The Carlisle State Brewery was established, half the pubs were closed and managers exercised strict control in the remainder. Government control lasted for over half a century.

With the grouping of 1st January 1923, the Maryport & Carlisle, LNWR, Caledonian, G&SW and Midland became part of the London Midland & Scottish Railway (LMS) whilst the North Eastern and North British were absorbed by the London & North Eastern Railway (LNER).

These two massive companies soon introduced new locomotive classes, some of which were characteristic of Citadel until the 1960s. Particularly impressive were the LMS Stanier Coronation Pacifics, entrusted with most principal West Coast expresses, and the LNER Gresley A3 Pacifics, which worked fast services to and from Edinburgh Waverley.

Nationalisation of the railways on 1st January 1948 saw the LMS and the LNER taken over by British Railways (BR). However, in some respects the Border City reverted to its pre-grouping 'frontier' days. The Scottish Region and London Midland Region met here, and North Eastern Region engines worked in from Newcastle. During the 1950s, BR began to change the old order at Carlisle. In 1951 a certain amount of resignalling took place and a modern box was built to control the southern approaches to the station. Then, eight years later, work began on Kingmoor New Yard, a massive venture designed to replace several of the antiquated yards around the city.

On 27th March 1963, Beeching's notorious report 'The Reshaping of Britain's Railways' was published - ironically about the same time Kingmoor New Yard came into use. Implications for Carlisle included the demise of the Silloth branch, the end of most remaining wayside stations and their associated stopping trains, and the closure of virtually all rural goods yards. A belated victim of this rationalisation was the Waverley route to Edinburgh, in 1969. Steam traction had been phased out in 1967 amid scenes of unprecedented and almost manic attention from enthusiasts.

Carlisle's industrial base was changing as well; Cowans Sheldon was taken over in 1970 and the State Brewery was sold off in 1972. Electrification of the West Coast main line through Carlisle was completed in 1974, but by this time the parallel M6 motorway was already providing severe competition. The former G&SW and Midland routes had become poor relations and the bland blue and grey corporate BR livery was everywhere. By 1977 Kingmoor New Yard was an important centre on the Speedlink network but a significant amount of the complex had already been shut down.

Rather than end this introduction on a gloomy note, it is appropriate to look back at the exciting days of steam-hauled expresses through Carlisle. W.A.C. Smith made a memorable journey back to Glasgow from the Border City on 12th July 1964: *'Ex-LNER class A2/3 Pacific No.60522 STRAIGHT DEAL waited in one of the centre roads at Citadel to take over the twelve-coach Sunday afternoon down express from Liverpool and Manchester to Glasgow. The train, Class 5 hauled and running late, duly arrived but presented myself and a fellow enthusiast with a difficult choice - Coronation Pacific No.46244 KING GEORGE VI was rostered for the down 'Royal Scot' which was scheduled to leave shortly afterwards. We opted for the former, fortunately as it turned out. During their short stay at Polmadie, the A2s earned no great reputation, but on this occasion No.60522 performed exceptionally well.*

Leaving 41 minutes late at 5.09pm, the engine made a flying start, enveloping our leading coach (appropriately a Thompson vehicle) in smoke and cinders. Gretna was passed in 10 minutes, then there was a brief pause at Ecclefechan where Mogul No.76090 passed on a ballast train. Blowing off furiously, the loco ran into Lockerbie, still 41 minutes down, but despite a double draw being necessary and a bout of slipping, we got away 39 minutes late. Fairburn 2-6-4T No.42693 came on at Beattock to bank us, and the climb was made in a very respectable 14 minutes.

Carstairs was reached 24 minutes late, but 10 minutes were spent taking water as an English Electric Type 4 diesel took over the three Edinburgh coaches. Departure was 30 minutes late and Motherwell was reached 28 minutes down. However, the 3 minute booked stop was cut to 1 minute and Glasgow Central was reached only 19 minutes late at 7.29pm, after a splendid trip behind a steam engine in its twilight days.'

5

Resplendent North Eastern 4-4-0 No.1929 (later LNER class D17/2) stands in the company's bay platform at Citadel around 1914.

Former North British Atlantic No.9906 TERIBUS passes Carlisle No.5 box and Crown Street goods depot as it approaches Citadel with a train from Newcastle, around 1930. The coaches are a mixture of Midland, North Eastern and North British designs. At the time, several of these impressive engines were working from London Road shed, having been superseded on top link Waverley route duties at Canal by Gresley Pacifics. The name TERIBUS was derived from the Hawick town motto. Photograph J.J. Cunningham.

Chapter 2
NORTH EASTERN

The Pennines stretch from Derbyshire to the Cheviots and there are few gaps in the backbone of England. Any hint of lower ground therefore assumed considerable importance as a means of communication between the east and west coasts. Fortunately, a way through the hills exists between Newcastle and Carlisle, comprising the Tyne valley on the Northumberland side and an ill-defined watershed between Haltwhistle and Gilsland near the Cumberland border. The latter is around the 500ft mark and was created by Pennine glaciers pushing westwards towards the Irish Sea. Roman occupation forces appreciated the significance of this gap and drew the boundary roughly along the line of it. In AD 122-126 Emperor Hadrian built his wall from the mouth of the Tyne to the Solway Firth and enhanced it with a ditch, or *vallum* on either side, as well as milecastles and forts at regular intervals.

As the Northumberland coalfield developed, better transport facilities to the west coast became imperative. During the 1790s several proposals for a canal from Newcastle to Maryport emerged, but all of them foundered. Then in 1799 a lengthy wagonway through the Tyne gap was suggested. The success of the Carlisle Canal - opened in 1823 - revived interest at the Newcastle end. There was much debate about the respective merits of canals and railways, but this was a couple of years before the Stockton & Darlington line made its mark. Eventually cash proved the decisive factor, for in October 1824 a report revealed that a canal would cost almost four times as much as a railway. Furthermore, William Chapman, who had been a champion of the waterway scheme, now recommended laying rails instead.

A decision to build the railway was made in March 1825 and George Stephenson carried out the necessary survey. On 22nd May 1829 the Newcastle & Carlisle company gained parliamentary approval for a line from the west side of Newcastle to the canal basin at Carlisle, the Act specifically banning the use of locomotives. A ceremony to mark the laying of the first stone of Wetheral viaduct took place in March 1830 as a prelude to construction work on the 61 mile line, but subsequent progress was somewhat drawn out. A few years later the project received government finance via the Public Works Loan Commissioners, a scheme

ROMAN FRONTIER

A pair of new Metro-Cammell four-car diesel sets with buffet facilities, forming a Newcastle service on 31st August 1957. The train is standing at Platform 6, the former North Eastern bay at Citadel. Photograph W.A.C. Smith.

An Illustrated History of Carlisle's Railways

This diesel multiple unit seems to be making a decent attempt to revive the days before the North Eastern was admitted to Citadel! The Derby twin set, forming the Railway Enthusiasts Club 'Carlisle Goods Line Tour', stands in London Road goods shed on 10th September 1960. Photograph W.A.C. Smith.

Ex-North British 4-4-0s (mainly Scotts allocated to Canal) worked over the Newcastle & Carlisle line quite regularly in the 1930s. But this particular example - preserved No.256 GLEN DOUGLAS - was exploring certain backwaters as far as such passenger engines were concerned. The loco is approaching London Road Junction on 6th April 1963 with a railtour about to cover the Carlisle goods lines, Kingmoor New Yard, the Langholm branch and the Longtown - Gretna line. Photograph W.A.C. Smith.

which only assisted railways from 1837 to 1842. Afterwards, private capital was deemed adequate.

The Newcastle & Carlisle was planned as a public railway with tolls, like the Stockton & Darlington, but by the time the Hexham - Blaydon section opened in March 1835 it was operated as a private line. Steam locomotive design had improved markedly, so the company ordered three engines in anticipation of parliament abolishing the clause banning them. This had not happened when services began, so the prohibition was completely ignored! A gentleman by the name of Bacon Grey was not amused and obtained an injunction to stop the trains, but public opinion was behind the Newcastle & Carlisle and traffic resumed. In June 1835 parliament made the use of locomotives official.

In June 1836 trains began to use the Haydon Bridge - Hexham stretch and on 19th July 1836 the line between Carlisle London Road and Greenhead came into use. The latter event was watched by a huge crowd and there was a public holiday in Carlisle. There were hitches; a coupling broke leaving the carriage conveying the Mayor and Corporation of Carlisle stranded until their absence was noted! Blaydon to Gateshead opened in March 1837 and the first railway across the width of England was finally completed on 18th June 1838, when the gap between Greenhead and Haydon Bridge was plugged.

Celebrations on this occasion were the most spectacular so far. There were five return trains from Carlisle to Newcastle and no less than thirteen in the opposite direction. Some 3,500 passengers were carried and all fourteen locomotives owned by the company were pressed into service, the longest train consisting of nineteen coaches hauled by the appropriately named GOLIATH. The Newcastle contingent did not begin to return from Carlisle until 10pm, and a collision delayed matters further. Eventually the last special steamed into Gateshead at 6am, after a thunderstorm had soaked passengers in the open coaches. It was a memorable day in more than one respect! In the meantime, on 9th March 1837, a branch had opened from a junction just outside London Road station to the Carlisle Canal basin. Initially the waterway and railway managements co-operated to their mutual benefit. Coal destined for Ireland flowed from pits around Greenhead and there was even goods traffic from distant Baltic ports. Passenger services became more convenient in 1839 when the line from Blaydon to Newcastle, along the north bank of the Tyne, came into operation. However, the Newcastle & Carlisle still favoured right-hand running, one of its many early eccentricities.

For a decade the first route across the Pennines was actually an important outlet to the south, although the flow of traffic varied as new lines opened. From 1838 Tyneside passengers used Newcastle & Carlisle trains, the Carlisle - Preston stagecoach, then the West Coast railway south of Preston to travel to London. When the East Coast route arrived at Gateshead in 1844, it was the turn of Carlisle passengers bound for Euston to head east. A through journey of 13 hours via Newcastle, York and Rugby was soon possible. Such adventures ebbed away when the Lancaster & Carlisle opened in 1846. From 1st August 1848 the Newcastle & Carlisle became part of George Hudson's empire, but reverted to its original management on 1st January 1850. By this time it was merely a cross-country route, albeit an important one.

From around 70ft above sea level at Carlisle, the Newcastle line climbed for twelve miles to a 494ft summit east of Narworth. With gradients as steep as 1 in 129 many eastbound freights needed banking assistance. The obvious route from the Solway lowlands to Gilsland was along the Irthling valley past Brampton, but Lord Carlisle only supported the project on condition that it connected with his private colliery wagonway at Milton

8

The North Eastern approach to Carlisle, originally the Canal branch and also used by Midland trains from 1876. In summer 1953 Gateshead B1 4-6-0 No.61199 heads out of the city with the 3.55pm to Newcastle. London Road yard is on the right. Photograph J.W. Armstrong Trust.

(which later became Brampton Junction). Consequently, the railway found itself picking a way through broken and somewhat remote country in the Pennine foothills. This stretch of track was also characterised by twenty or so abrupt curves, typical of earlier horse-operated lines.

Immediately after leaving London Road the line bridged the River Petteril and headed eastwards through Scotby to Wetheral (4¼ miles from Citadel). Just beyond here the River Eden flowed in a deeply incised valley, and a 95ft high viaduct consisting of five arches, each with an 80ft span, was necessary to cross it. Less than half a mile further on, a tributary valley was conquered by Corby viaduct, comprising seven 40ft arches with a maximum height of 70ft. These were monumental engineering works for the mid-1830s.

Near Hayton a landowner forced the line to deviate south-eastwards into the Cowran Hills. In order to maintain a reasonable gradient for the proposed horse traction, a lengthy cutting punctuated by a bridge over the River Gelt was created between Skellian and Hell Beck. The mile-long western section was up to 110ft deep, a record for the time, and as gentle slopes were necessary to avoid landslips the excavation was 300ft wide at its deepest point. Normally a tunnel would have been bored through a barrier of this magnitude, but numerous underground springs rendered one impossible, so a million cubic yards of subsoil had to be removed instead.

Beyond Brampton Junction (11 miles) the line was easier to build but the country became much wilder, the ground rising towards 2,041ft Cold Fell five miles away to the south. At Gilsland (17¾ miles) a sweeping curve took the rails across the course of Hadrian's Wall twice in quick succession. After Greenhead (19¾ miles) a descent alongside Tipalt Burn led to the South Tyne valley and Haltwhistle (23 miles). Gradients for westbound trains were much easier than those out of the Solway lowlands, the maximum being 1 in 264.

Newcastle & Carlisle station buildings were neat, practical and completely in keeping with their surroundings. They also represented the first real attempt to create an overall style for a railway of some length. John Dobson, the renowned Newcastle architect, was credited with certain major bridges on the line, although it is more likely that Benjamin Green designed the stations. He was only in his mid-twenties, but was already helping Dobson with the reconstruction of central Newcastle. The buildings were mainly two-storey blocks with dressed-stone walls and slate roofs. A cross gable was corbelled out at first floor level to form a projecting centrepiece, whilst the moulded widow hoods and chimneys were treated in Tudor fashion. Greenhead, Gilsland and Milton (Brampton Junction) displayed the style admirably.

Haltwhistle was more substantial and featured prominent gables, both large and small, together with clusters of chimneys. London Road had a Tudor office block set no less than twenty yards from the departure line across intervening sidings. In fact most buildings were some distance from the rails and some were not even parallel to the tracks. There were no platforms at first and when provided they tended to look generous, a feature still apparent today. Charming little canopies adorned the stations in Newcastle & Carlisle days, but larger, clumsy ones were provided by the North Eastern Railway.

Several stations on the line had a claim to fame. On the negative side, Gilsland (Rosehill until 1869) was built near the site of Roman milecastle 48 and destroyed a stretch of Hadrian's Wall in the process. Narworth, a private station for the Earl of Carlisle until it appeared in the public timetable from 1871, was the site of an early road accident. In 1926 a new charabanc stalled on the level crossing and was struck by a Newcastle - Carlisle express resulting in eight fatalities. On the positive side, a booking clerk at Milton by the name of Edmondson grew

Pioneering Newcastle & Carlisle Railway engineering at its best. Gateshead B1 4-6-0 No.61014 ORIBI crosses the magnificent viaduct over the River Eden and enters Wetheral station with a Newcastle - Carlisle train on 16th August 1952. Photograph J.W. Armstrong Trust.

An Illustrated History of Carlisle's Railways

The wonderfully pedantic notice facing pedestrians intending to use the footpath incorporated in Wetheral viaduct. Did British Railways really need to inform people that the toll for their short walk was authorised by the Act of Parliament 10 Geo. IV Cap. 72? No doubt, it was an ancient legal requirement. Photograph J.W. Armstrong Trust.

Gateshead B1 4-6-0 No.61023 HIROLA rolls into Wetheral station with a Newcastle - Carlisle train on 16th August 1952. The footpath alongside Wetheral viaduct can be seen just beyond the plank crossing for barrows. An adjustment in platform level was necessary to accommodate the original Newcastle & Carlisle building and its delicate canopy. A fine North Eastern footbridge completes the scene. Photograph J.W. Armstrong Trust.

tired of filling in paper tickets and counterfoils with the number, date, time and destination. He had card tickets printed and devised a dispenser for issuing them. The management were impressed and adopted the new system. Other railways followed and Edmondson tickets became the norm throughout the world until computerisation during the last few decades.

The Newcastle & Carlisle paid dividends of up to 6 per cent throughout the 1840s and 1850s. It was ripe for picking by one of the railway giants and succumbed to the North Eastern on 17th July 1862 after four years of bitter fighting. Passenger trains from Newcastle were transferred to Carlisle Citadel on 1st January 1863. By this time two branches fed into the western half of the cross-Pennine line. A highly scenic single track route from Haltwhistle to the market town of Alston was authorised on 26th August 1846. It opened on 17th November 1852 and incorporated a spectacular viaduct across the South Tyne, at Lambley. The Brampton branch was a far more complex affair. In 1799 the Earl of Carlisle opened a wagonway from Lambley to Brampton serving his collieries en route. When the Carlisle-Greenhead section of the Newcastle & Carlisle opened in 1836 a junction was installed at Milton and horse-drawn carriages provided a connecting service along the line to Brampton. Steam engines were employed from 1881 but operations ceased after a Board of Trade inspection in 1890. It enjoyed a modest revival, as noted later.

The earliest locomotives to run into Carlisle were 0-4-0s supplied by Hawthorn of Newcastle for the opening of the Newcastle & Carlisle Railway. Under North Eastern auspices Fletcher 2-4-0s were employed, followed by McDonell 4-4-0s, Worsdell's very fine 4-4-0s and Raven Atlantics. Local trains to Brampton and Haltwhistle were worked by Fletcher BTP 0-4-4Ts for many years. After World War I 0-6-0s were joined by 0-8-0s for freight work. North Eastern passenger locomotives were painted light green lined with olive green, black and vermilion. Coaches were a rich shade of plum red set off with brown roofs.

In 1880, during enlargement of the station, NER trains were given their own bay platform at Citadel. By this time the Newcastle - Carlisle line was becoming one of the company's most important branches, at least in the northern division. In the early 1900s around 35 North Eastern trains were dealt with every weekday at Citadel. There was an overnight Newcastle - Stranraer express to connect with the Larne steamers and this was allowed just ninety minutes for the difficult road to Carlisle. Another fast journey was possible by early afternoon through coaches from Glasgow Central to

An unidentified ex-North Eastern class D20 4-4-0 stands at Wetheral with a Carlisle train on 16th August 1952. By this time it was unusual to see D20s on passenger turns over the Newcastle & Carlisle. Being a summer Saturday, Gateshead no doubt had to deploy its B1s on additional East Coast main line trains. With at least seven coaches in tow, this must have been a stiff challenge for the ageing D20. Photograph J.W. Armstrong Trust.

10

Newcastle. When the LNER took over in 1923 the timetable featured non-stop expresses leaving both Newcastle and Carlisle just after midnight. These conveyed mail, milk and through coaches for Stranraer, taking 75 minutes between the two cities. There were frequent daytime expresses calling at four or five intermediate stations, or just Haltwhistle and Hexham. A good local service was provided and this even applied on Sundays. In summer a Newcastle - Silloth train ran for holidaymakers, whilst pleasure traffic from Carlisle was generated by the sylvan delights of Wetheral, How Mill and Brampton.

During LNER days ex-North British locos off Canal shed began to appear on the former North Eastern line, whilst from 1935 class D49 4-4-0s became the mainstay of fast and semi-fast trains. Tyneside-based V1 2-6-2Ts also worked into Carlisle. As a result of road competition, a couple of steam railcars had already replaced the BTP 0-4-4Ts on local services. After World War 2, B1 4-6-0s began to appear, together with the occasional 2-6-0 and V2 2-6-2. Sometimes Gateshead shed even sent a Pacific across the Pennines. In 1957 diesel multiple units took over most services, although the Newcastle - Stranraer boat train remained loco-hauled until the 'Port Road' closed in 1965. Sprinters and Pacers now maintain the Carlisle - Newcastle service.

Above. Gateshead must have been really short of modern power on 16th August 1952. D20 4-4-0 No.62371 drifts into Wetheral with a Newcastle express, its safety valves just lifting to indicate a good head of steam for the climb through How Mill to Brampton. Timekeeping was probably not of the highest order and the engine was withdrawn just over two years later. Photograph J.W. Armstrong Trust.

Below. Brampton Junction, looking west in 1952. The line to Carlisle curves through the cutting on the left whilst a short stretch of the Brampton Town branch on the right was still in use as a siding. Photograph J.W. Armstrong Trust.

Inevitably, the North Eastern approach to Carlisle has lost its branches and most of its local stations. Passenger services returned to Brampton Town on 1st August 1913, although they were withdrawn again (as a wartime economy measure) on 1st March 1917. Another attempt was made between 1st March 1920 and 29th October 1923, but that proved the end and the line closed completely two months later. How Mill lost its passenger services on 5th January 1959, followed by Scotby on 2nd November 1959. Meanwhile there was still a reasonable service from Carlisle to Newcastle - sixteen departures on Saturdays in summer 1961, for example. Wetheral and Heads Nook closed on 2nd January 1967, but the saddest loss was the lovely Alston branch on 3rd May 1976. A modest revival came with the reopening of Wetheral on 5th October 1981.

Top right. B1 No.61014 ORIBI of Gateshead shed arrives at Haltwhistle with the 2.20pm from Newcastle to Carlisle on 12th April 1952. The delightful Tudor station building on the left dates from Newcastle & Carlisle Railway days. When it was withdrawn at the end of 1966, ORIBI was at North Blyth - an unlikely depot which was once the preserve of Q6s and J27s. Photograph J.W. Armstrong Trust.

Right. Ex-North Eastern G5 0-4-4T No.67315, the regular Alston branch engine for many years, stands in Haltwhistle station with the 3.30pm to Alston on 12th April 1952. It is in its usual spotless condition, the proud crew posing for the camera being cleaner Alwyn Hind (on the footplate), Driver Alan Robinson and Fireman Maurice Peart. A fine North Eastern signal box completes this evocative scene. Photograph J.W. Armstrong Trust.

Left. The clean lines of G5 0-4-4T No.67315 are emphasised by its sparkling paintwork in this view at Haltwhistle on 12th April 1952. Photograph J.W. Armstrong Trust.

Above. With the River South Tyne glistening on the left and the Newcastle & Carlisle line straight as a die on the right, a Metro-Cammell twin forming the 2.05pm to Alston awaits departure from Haltwhistle on 28th September 1963. Photograph W.A.C. Smith.

Below. Class K1 2-6-0 No.62026 of Blaydon shed thunders past Border Counties Junction just west of Hexham with a freight for Carlisle London Road yard on 12th April 1952. The Border Counties line, through wild and beautiful Kielder Forest to Riccarton Junction on the Waverley route, branches off to the left. Border Counties box also controlled the Allendale branch, thus the third signal post overlooking the River Tyne. But this line closed completely in 1950, so perhaps there had been some delay with track lifting. Photograph J.W. Armstrong Trust.

Above. A Whitehaven train at Citadel in 1953, with Workington 2P 4-4-0 No.40694 in charge. By this time the Maryport & Carlisle bay had become platform No.2. The ex-LMS corridor coaches were one of the 'M&C Narrow Sets', standard vehicles with all drop windows barred and guards' lookouts removed because of very tight bridge clearances. A few years previously, Workington shed had received a couple of brand new Ivatt 4MT 2-6-0s for hauling West Cumberland passenger trains. Photograph Neville Stead Collection.

Below. Citadel in sunshine on 31st May 1951 and even the grimy gothic glazing looked quite cheerful on this lazy, hot afternoon. Stanier 2-6-4T No.42544 idles away the time at Platform 2, awaiting departure with the 1.25pm for Whitehaven. Photograph H.C. Casserley.

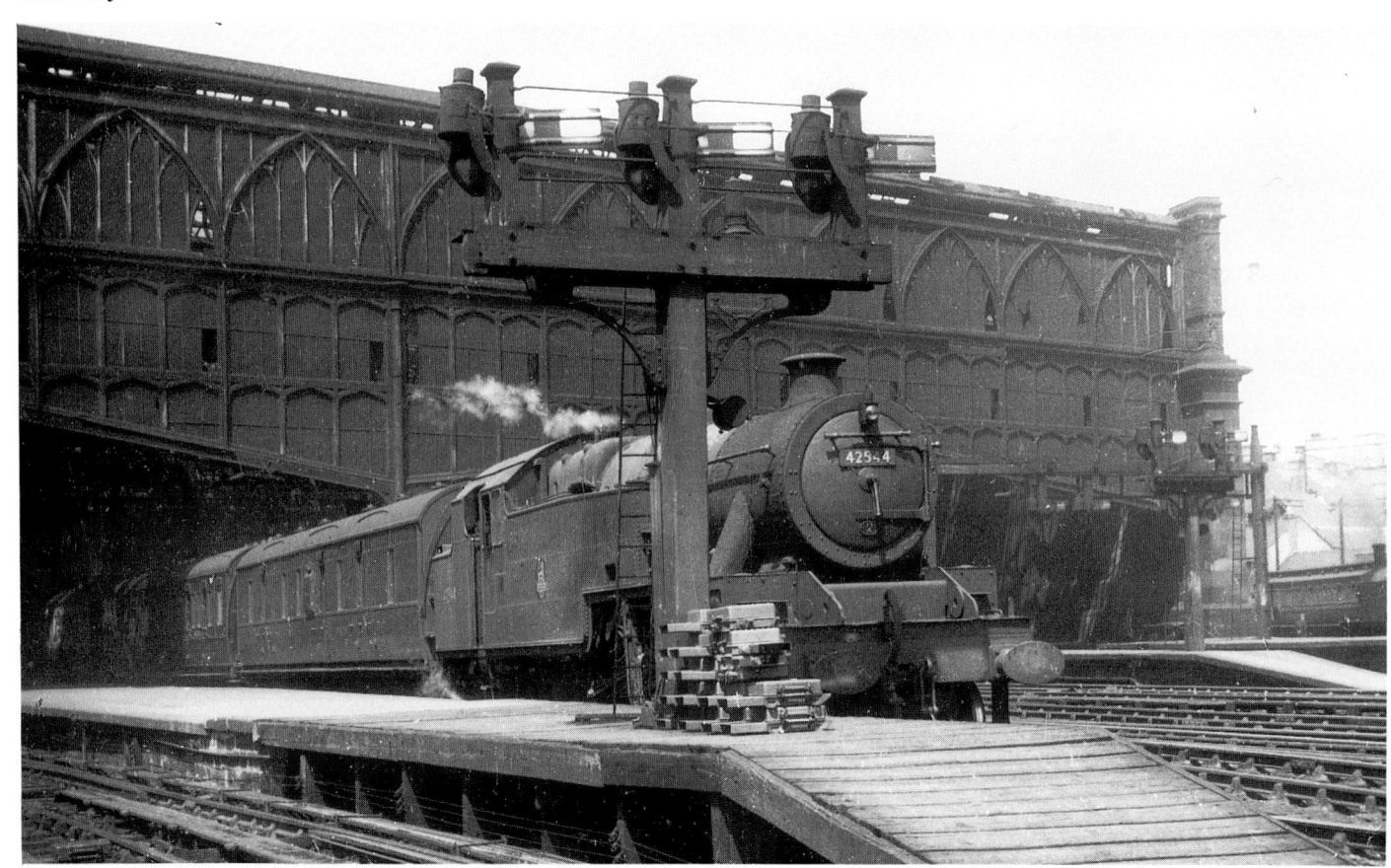

Chapter 3
MARYPORT & CARLISLE

Coal was being worked at Mealsgate near Wigton as early as 1567 and by the early 1700s there were several pits in the Ellen valley south of Aspatria. Unfortunately this part of the West Cumberland coalfield suffered from its isolation. At the time, coal travelling some distance was transported by sea, but the loading facilities at nearby Allonby were woefully inadequate. Consequently Humphrey Senhouse (of Netherhall) decided to build a harbour and settlement at the mouth of the River Ellen. Maryport, named after his wife, was one of the earliest examples of a planned industrial town in Britain.

In 1750 there were just two houses alongside the new haven, but growth was rapid; an ironworks was established during 1752 and a two-mile wagonway from the mines on Broughton Moor opened in 1755. Twenty years later the population had reached 1,300. During the 1830s some 100,000 tons of coal was being exported through Maryport annually and the grid of streets with their red sandstone buildings was well established. By then the town was home for almost 4,000 people. Elsewhere on the Cumbrian coast, Workington and Whitehaven were flourishing as a result of coal and iron, whilst Wigton was weaving checks and ginghams for Carlisle's textile factories.

In the mid-1830s a later Humphrey Senhouse suggested a railway from Maryport to Carlisle. Further south, the rival Lowther family of Whitehaven had plans for a similar but longer line. The latter scheme foundered, leaving a clear path for the Maryport & Carlisle Railway. George Stephenson was commissioned to survey the route and issued his preliminary report in October 1836.

It was glowingly optimistic. The renowned engineer stated that competing lines were unlikely to be built and the route would remain 'the great thoroughfare' for this part of Cumberland. It was a prophesy that turned out to be entirely correct, despite the complex, fickle and sometimes cut-throat railway developments over the ensuing ninety years. When the Maryport & Carlisle was absorbed by the LMS in 1923, only the Great Western had a longer pedigree.

The railway acquired its Act on 12th July 1837. Shares were snapped up, subscribers believing that their line would form a link between Europe and Ireland in conjunction with the Newcastle & Carlisle. However, the late 1830s saw a slump in the wake of the 'Little Railway Mania' of 1836. Shares were forfeited and construction was painfully slow as a result of the lack of cash. One contractor sued the company because interfering officials failed to deliver materials, an ominous sign of incompetent management. In 1839 Stephenson recommended the Cumbrian coast option for the proposed London - Glasgow trunk route, but this was re-

JOHN PEEL COUNTRY

After the War there was a conspicuous lack of glazing at the south end of Citadel and during heavy rain it was as wet under the overall roof as at the platform ends. In a downpour on 16th April 1953, Stanier tank No.42544 eases into the Maryport & Carlisle bay with the 9.55am from Whitehaven. Photograph H.C. Casserley.

An Illustrated History of Carlisle's Railways

With the bulk of Citadel on the left, a West Cumberland train leaves Carlisle on a sunny Edwardian afternoon. No.18, an 0-6-0 built by the North British Locomotive Co. in Glasgow during 1908, had become No.14293 by the time it was withdrawn in 1925. The engine must have been new when this view was taken, for the varnished teak coach livery had only partially given way to the gold-lined dark green and greenish white finish, introduced in 1905.

jected. Shortly afterwards, he terminated his involvement with the Maryport & Carlisle, no doubt fearful of being associated with an utter failure.

The first seven miles of track from South Quay at Maryport to Arkleby pits opened on 5th July 1840. This was followed by the short stretch to Aspatria on 12th April 1841, accompanied by a passenger service of five trains each way calling at Bulgill and Arkleby. Attention then turned to the northern end, and a 12 mile section from Wigton to a junction with the Newcastle & Carlisle Canal branch at the Bog, opened on 10th May 1843. A station, probably little more than a wooden shed, was provided at Bogfield and saw two departures and arrivals a day. Trains called at temporary halts at Dalston and Currock Pool, and ornate stations at Crofton, Curthwaite and Cummersdale were promised. Wigton to Brookfield (less than a mile) and Aspatria to Low Row (just over three miles) came into operation on 2nd December 1844. The gap between them was finally closed on 10th February 1845 'an event that in local eyes must have equalled the driving of the last spike on the Canadian Pacific' to quote railway historian David Joy!

Northumbrian coal flowed along the line from the outset and another company extended rails south to Workington and Whitehaven in 1846-47. Prosperity should have been assured, but the Maryport & Carlisle was going through a decade of chaos. Most spectacular was the saga of Crown Street. In 1843 the company commissioned the acclaimed Newcastle architect John Dobson to design a grand classical terminus at Carlisle. When the Lancaster & Carlisle was authorised in 1844 and a London - Glasgow trunk route looked imminent, Dobson advised the local company to save its money. Nevertheless, on 30th December 1844 the Maryport board opened a trailing connection off the Newcastle & Carlisle to a rudimentary station in Crown Street. This was all very well until an Anglo-Scottish alliance comprising the Lancaster & Carlisle and Caledonian, became a reality. These two concerns had chosen a site at Court Square for their joint station and the terminus at Crown Street formed part of it.

Eventually the Maryport & Carlisle agreed to release the land for £7,000, but matters became complicated when George Hudson leased the West Cumberland line on 1st October 1848 and demanded £100,000 for the property. Trains from Maryport to Crown Street fouled the main line three times, causing some inconvenience. Hudson received a substantially enhanced payment for the site but still refused to surrender it, so the Lancaster & Carlisle gained legal possession of the terminus and promptly demolished it. On 17th March 1849 a hundred men armed with picks and crowbars descended on the station after a morning train had departed and by noon the platforms, buildings, goods yard and approach line were no more. From the following day Maryport trains terminated at London Road.

By this time Hudson's fortunes were in decline and he relinquished control of the Maryport & Carlisle on 1st January 1850, but the railway was in a chronic state of confusion. Staff drunkenness was rife, senior officers took time off at will and a previous company secretary had spent time in jail. A Commission of Investigation was appointed and soon discovered that £200,000 had been borrowed illegally, unnecessary expenses had been incurred, and high fares went hand in hand with grossly inefficient working. Even the 1844 *Bradshaw* had described a certain train as 'occasionally at 10 o'clock'! In November 1850 the chairman and five directors were replaced and a gradual improvement began.

Class 4F 0-6-0 No.44511 sends a cloud of smoke towards the council houses of Currock estate as it approaches Cummersdale on 2nd August 1954. The train is the 7.50pm from Carlisle to Whitehaven, rostered for a 2P 4-4-0. However, Workington 4Fs were not uncommon on West Cumberland passenger trains. Photograph Robert Leslie.

16

Bathed in evening sunshine on 18th September 1954, Class 5 4-6-0 No.45141 darkens the sky as it leaves Dalston with the 5.08pm from Carlisle to Whitehaven. An Upperby 2-6-4T was the normal motive power for this working. Photograph Robert Leslie.

Firstly, the arrangements at Carlisle were sorted out. An agreement was finally reached with the Lancaster & Carlisle and Caledonian, allowing Maryport trains access to Citadel from 1st June 1851 via a connection off the erstwhile route to Crown Street. A more convenient curve from Forks Junction west of Bogfield opened on 8th August 1852. Although services from the Cumbrian coast subsequently mingled with West coast expresses, the Maryport & Carlisle was very much a poor relation at the main line station.

John Addison was Secretary, Manager and Engineer from 1857 to 1884 and under his guidance the company became extremely prosperous. Dividends on shares climbed steadily from 1864 and reached a remarkable 13 per cent in 1873, a level surpassed only by a couple of South Wales valley lines. This enviable state of affairs was almost entirely due to the burgeoning West Cumberland coal and iron industry, coupled with exemplary management. But Maryport itself was far too dependent on minerals and this eventually proved its undoing.

The 1860s and 1870s were decades of expansion for the railway. Track penetrated further into Maryport harbour during 1860 and a new passenger station was provided nearer the town centre at the same time. No expense was spared on this building, which incorporated the company's head office. Apparently the chairman expressed fears that shareholders might regard it as 'rather too handsome a station', but no criticism was forthcoming. By 1861 the whole of the main line had been doubled. A loop between Aspatria and Wigton opened in 1866 to tap the northern tip of the coalfield around Mealsgate, whilst the Derwent branch from Bulgill to Brigham on the Workington - Cockermouth line was completed during 1867. Finally, a new curve from Currock Junction to the Citadel approach tracks opened on 7th July 1877. This was necessary because of major changes associated with the goods avoiding lines.

Shortly after leaving Citadel, trains bound for Maryport veered south away from the main line and squealed round the reverse curve to Currock Junction. At Cummersdale they crossed a skew bridge over the River Caldew and began to head south westwards, climbing steadily up the valley side to Dalston (4½ miles). A westward course over Cardew mires took the track to almost 150 feet before a descent to just below 100 feet at Crofton. This level was maintained

Class 5 4-6-0 No.45108 plods through Dalston with the mid-morning goods from Carlisle to West Cumberland on 22nd August 1956. The first five vehicles are empty milk tanks bound for the creamery at Aspatria. Photograph Robert Leslie.

Having topped the rise of 1 in 300 up the Caldew valley, Workington 4F 0-6-0 No.44510 storms through Dalston with the evening goods from Carlisle to Barrow in Furness on 4th August 1954. The fireman leans out of his cab to catch the breeze at the end of this hot sunny Cumberland day. Note the cattle dock on the left and a small oil terminal in the centre background. Photograph Robert Leslie.

through undulating terrain consisting of drumlins and other Ice Age debris from the Lake District, together with sudden glacial meltwater channels. At Wigton (11¾ miles) rising ground forced the line to climb again, for about a mile.

A bridge across the River Waver was followed by isolated Leegate station. To the south, almost empty countryside stretched away to Mealsgate, the Caldbeck Fells, Skiddaw and the heart of Lakeland. Beyond Brayton trains breasted a summit of nearly 200 feet before the descent to sea level began. From Aspatria (20¼ miles) the obvious route was down the fairly deep Ellen valley, railway and river keeping close company all the way to the coast. This was a remote passage despite a couple of collieries alongside the line, for neither Bulgill nor Dearham stations were particularly convenient for the farming villages on adjacent ridges. By the time the train reached Maryport (27¾ miles) it had passed beneath 38 overbridges, crossed 33 underbridges and threaded six miles of cutting since leaving Carlisle.

Maryport & Carlisle stations displayed on intriguing collection of buildings, almost invariably of rich red sandstone. The original structure at Aspatria (1841) was a gem. It consisted of a tall single-storey block parallel to the track and a cross-gable projecting on to the platform placed slightly asymmetrically. The roofs in bluish-green slates had a very steep pitch and featured dormer windows. Prominent octagonal chimneys rose from a plinth at the apex of each gable, whilst authentic Tudor windows with angular dripstones were provided. There were also some delightful details, notably the little projections below each chimney plinth, supported by a corbel in the form of a human head with a sombre face.

Such architectural indulgence had to go as times became harder. Wigton (1843) and Curthwaite (1844) were both provided with a two-storey house and low

Upperby 2P No.40695 casts a long shadow as it leans into the curve at the approach to Dalston with the 4.15pm from Whitehaven to Carlisle, on the lovely autumn evening of 18th September 1954. The coaches were a mixed bunch, but all had the mandatory window bars. Varied motive power on these West Cumberland trains included Ivatt 2MT 2-6-0s based at Workington for the Cockermouth, Keswick & Penrith line and, on at least one occasion, a Carlisle Jubilee. Photograph Robert Leslie.

Wigton station on 17th May 1969. A 2-car dmu arrives during the first part of its lengthy scenic trek from Carlisle to Barrow. These Derby railcars had just replaced 'Lightweight' dmu's, but barred windows were still a feature. The delightful Maryport & Carlisle footbridge and slightly disappointing amenities block appear to be in the middle of open country, but the busy Cumberland market town is just off to the right. Photograph Paul Anderson.

amenity block on the platform. Embellishment was minimal, although enough cash was found for a pointed gothic arch over certain doorways. Leegate and Dearham Bridge (both 1845) reflected a company deep in the doldrums. They could have been crofters' cottages and were completely devoid of decoration.

Wealthy landowners had a strong influence on Maryport & Carlisle affairs and one outcome was the erection of two highly attractive private stations. Brayton (1844) served Brayton Hall, seat of Sir Wilfrid Lawson who later became chairman of the company. The building had much in common with that at Aspatria, although paired chimneys and a lower profile gave it a charm of its own. Crofton (1856), provided for the Brisco family of Crofton Hall, was unlike any other on the line. It was constructed of cream limestone and featured twin pavilions, a bay window and slit windows in the gable ends.

The *tour de force* was undoubtedly Maryport (1860) where an immensely long assemblage rambled along the single platform. The structure consisted of a pair of very tall two-storey houses, the southern one having a transverse appendage, with a lower block stretching between them. Early 1840s practice was resurrected by the use of steeply-pitched roofs and Tudor trappings. Gable ends were finished off with slender finials and rather thin chimneys were arranged in groups of two, three or four. But the overpowering feature was a massive tower, defiantly castellated, adorned with large clock faces, and capped by a stumpy spire.

During its independent existence the Maryport & Carlisle owned a total of sixty locomotives which entered service in ones and twos between 1840 and 1921. They were an incredibly mixed bunch; in fact the largest class consisted of just three similar engines. No less than ten builders were involved - Tulk & Ley, Hawthorn, Sharp Stewart, Richardson, E B Wilson, Beyer Peacock, Neilson, North British Loco, Yorkshire Engine Co. and the company's own Maryport works. There were tender, side tank and saddle tank variants, whilst wheel arrangements comprised 2-2-2, 4-2-0, 0-4-0, 0-4-2, 0-4-4,

A Carlisle - Whitehaven train calls at Aspatria on 5th July 1969, by which time the station had become an unstaffed halt. The waiting rooms on the right were built in 1861 when this section of the Maryport & Carlisle was doubled, but the remarkable 1841 block still dominated the other platform, despite later accretions. Even the chimneys were fair representations of those found on locomotives! Until 1930, connecting services for Mealsgate veered off to the right in the distance. Photograph Paul Anderson.

2-4-0 and 0-6-0 types. At Citadel, Maryport & Carlisle trains had a delightfully parochial air about them. For instance, 29 and 30 were the highest running numbers ever used on locos and that was as late as 1921. Engines were painted a deep shade of green relieved by black bands lined with vermilion. Coaches were finished in varnished teak until 1905 when a more colourful livery of dark green lower panels and white upper bodywork with gold lining was adopted. From the mid-1840s the principal engine shed was at Bogfield in Carlisle, but during 1876 this was replaced by larger facilities at nearby Currock.

Passenger services developed steadily from five each way in 1877 to seven in 1883 and eight in 1910, by which time the company was running combined rail and coach excursions to the Lake District. When the Maryport & Carlisle lost its independence in 1923 a record nine timetabled passenger trains ran in each direction, but great changes were in store as far as motive power was concerned. The LMS inherited 33 locos, but being non-standard no less than 25 of them had been withdrawn within six years and the last was scrapped in 1934. Fowler 2P 4-4-0s steadily took over passenger trains during this period. Currock shed proved another early casualty, closing in 1923, and Maryport works was also shut down. By the 1930s the town of Maryport was in deep recession, its pits idle or slack, the ironworks abandoned and unemployment at the staggering rate of almost 70 per cent.

From the late 1940s Stanier 2-6-4Ts from Upperby shed took over Cumbrian coast passenger trains and these were followed by large and small Ivatt 2-6-0s. Shortly after BR absorbed the LMS in 1948 attention turned to uneconomic stations, with the result that Curthwaite, Leegate, Brayton and Dearham Bridge closed in June 1950, followed by Cummersdale in June 1951. Passenger services had already been withdrawn from Wigton to Mealsgate in 1921, between Aspatria and Mealsgate in 1930 and along the Bullgill - Brigham branch in 1935.

Derby Lightweight diesel multiple units took over Carlisle - Whitehaven services on 7th February 1955 and the timetable was improved. In summer 1960, for instance, Maryport had sixteen departures from Carlisle on Mondays to Fridays. However, Bulgill station closed in March of that year. Derby Heavyweight dmus were introduced in 1968-69 and these maintained passenger services until the advent of Sprinters and Pacers. No doubt the Maryport & Carlisle board would be pleased that their line still had approximately fifteen trains each way a century and a half after it was completed.

Stations for the aristocracy 1: Brayton opened in December 1844 for the convenience of Sir Wilfred Lawson MP, Chairman of the Maryport & Carlisle from 1874 to 1906 and resident of nearby Brayton Hall. Although the station stood in splendid isolation north of Aspatria, it was also made available to the general public and actually became the terminus of Solway Junction trains from Kirtlebridge via the Solway Viaduct. The delectable little red sandstone building closed to passengers on 5th June 1950, although goods traffic continued until 27th September 1965. It was demolished just after this view was taken on 17th May 1969. Photograph Paul Anderson.

Stations for aristocracy 2: Crofton opened early in 1856 for the exclusive use of the Brisco family of nearby Crofton Hall, and did not appear in the public timetable. In any case, Curthwaite station was just a mile away. The goods yard closed on 15th December 1946 and it is almost certain that 'the nobs' had ceased to grace the platforms by this date. Although the cream stone building was unlike any other on the line, those 'ears' at the eaves were a characteristic Maryport & Carlisle feature. This view was taken on 5th July 1969. Photograph Paul Anderson.

With the monumental station towering about it, a Carlisle train waits at Maryport around 1910. A brisk wind from the Irish Sea whips steam from the safety valves of Maryport & Carlisle 2-4-0 No.R1. The engine was built at Maryport during 1867 as No.19, but was put on the duplicate list in 1884 when an 0-6-0 with the same number emerged from the company's works. Photograph courtesy R.M. Casserley

A Whitehaven - Carlisle train pauses at Maryport's long single platform on 26th April 1969. The houses of Netherton form a backdrop to the left, Maryport itself being away to the right. By this time the bulky tower forming the centrepiece of the station had long disappeared. Photograph Paul Anderson.

On 8th July 1969 Maryport station still displayed some of the confidence and affluence of the Maryport & Carlisle Railway in its heyday, despite having been partially demolished and virtually abandoned. The 1860 building in dark red sandstone featured many Tudor touches, notably the rather lean chimneys. Photograph Paul Anderson.

A pair of LNWR 'Claughton' 4-6-0s, No.2416 and No.1407 L/CPL. J.A. CHRISTIE VC climb away from Citadel with a ten-coach Glasgow - Euston express in the early 1920s.

Two 'Royal Scots' making an impressive sight at Citadel, probably in the late 1920s just after they were built. No.6118 ROYAL WELCH FUSILIER stands in the centre road while No.6123 ROYAL IRISH FUSILIER is ready to take an express south over the former LNWR main line.

Chapter 4
LONDON & NORTH WESTERN

There was optimistic talk of a railway from London to Birmingham and Lancashire as early as 1822, but at the time it must have seemed hopelessly over-ambitious. However, the Stockton & Darlington came on the scene in 1825 and prospered, then the Liverpool & Manchester opened in 1830 and proved a huge success. The latter gave rise to a flurry of promotion three years later and 6th May 1833 proved to be a momentous day in the history of Britain's railways. It was the occasion when both the London & Birmingham and Grand Junction (Birmingham to Warrington) acquired their Acts of Parliament. The latter opened in 1837 and the former was completed during 1838. Furthermore, the North Union Railway carried the tracks on to Preston in 1838 and the Lancaster & Preston Junction opened during 1840.

Back in 1835, at the end of the fever which gave rise to the London - Preston line, there were dreams about a trunk route to Glasgow and Edinburgh. Many miles of wilderness lay ahead, but at least there was some railway activity at Carlisle, in the form of the Newcastle and Maryport projects. Joseph Locke, chief engineer of the Grand Junction, produced a report in January 1836 recommending a route to Carlisle via the Lune Valley, Shap and Penrith. George Stephenson backed a plan for a line round the Cumbrian coast via Morecambe Bay, Ulverston, Whitehaven and Maryport. In November 1839 Robert Peel's government decided to appoint commissioners to examine the rival proposals and bring some order to the clearly needed Anglo - Scottish line. They opted for Locke's route with a modification so that it passed close to Kendal which had been agitating for a railway. The commissioners considered that there was only enough potential traffic for one railway between England and Scotland. George Hudson thought otherwise - by 1841 his embryo East Coast route had reached Darlington, the line to Gateshead was under construction two years later, and plans for an extension to Berwick were being formulated.

The race for Scotland was on. Despite the recession of the early 1840s, enough money had been raised for the Lancaster & Carlisle Railway, much of it from the companies already operating trains from London to Lancaster. A route through Milnthorpe, Oxenholme, Tebay and Penrith was determined, the Act being obtained on 6th June 1844 with only the Lancaster Canal lodging an objection.

SHAP ABBEY

Building a 69 mile line through very difficult terrain must have been a daunting prospect, but the directors pledged to complete it in just two years. Although single track was envisaged initially, the sensible decision to provide two sets of rails was made before construction began.

The Lancaster & Carlisle proved to be a classic example of early main line construction. Within a couple of weeks of parliamentary approval hundreds of navvies had been taken on and by January 1845 3,700 men, with 400 horses, had descended on the line. At the height of it, no less than 10,000 workers hacked and

A study in sunshine and shadows at Citadel in the mid-1950s. Fowler 'Patriot' 4-6-0 No.45547 is ready to leave with an up West Coast express. Photograph Neville Stead Collection.

An Illustrated History of Carlisle's Railways

Above. Three 'Coronation' Pacifics at Citadel in June 1956. On the left, No.46224 PRINCESS ALEXANDRA is at the head of the up 'Royal Scot', while No.46243 CITY OF LANCASTER on the right is in charge of a Glasgow Central - Birmingham New Street train. No.46250 CITY OF LICHFIELD waits on the up centre road with a special working. Photograph J.F. Ward Collection.

Below. By the early 1960s diesels had taken over many West Coast main line workings, but steam was still very much in evidence at Carlisle on other duties. English Electric Type 4 No.D216 ticks away in one of the main platform roads as an 0-6-0T, acting as station pilot, deals with a couple of Travelling Post Office vehicles. Photograph I.G. Holt.

shovelled away at rock and earth in Shap cutting, the Lune gorge and elsewhere. They were a mixture of English, Irish and Scots and the first two contingents clashed violently in the notorious Penrith riots. Back on site, injuries were frequent and several navvies were killed.

Considering the magnitude of the task, it is hardly surprising that the Lancaster & Carlisle did not meet its two year deadline for opening. Spells of labour shortage resulting from the demands of the railway mania did not help but the proprietors, it turned out, were not that far off the mark. Trains began running from Lancaster to Oxenholme on 22nd September 1846 and through services to Carlisle commenced three months later,

on 17th December. The proposed central station in Carlisle was still the subject of heated discussions, so for an uneasy nine months trains from the south had to use the Newcastle & Carlisle terminus at London Road. This was reached by means of a curve sanctioned on 21st June 1845 off the authorised route into Carlisle. A reversal into London Road was still necessary, but this mattered little as there were just two trains each way over the Lancaster & Carlisle at the time. A service for Birmingham left at 8am, followed by the 2.30pm for Euston which reached the capital at 5.32am. Arrivals were at 5.20pm and 11am respectively. In 1847 the first night mails battled over Shap during the early hours, headed by Crewe-type 2-2-2s

and 2-4-0s with names like WORDSWORTH, WINDERMERE and BELTED WILL.

Even when the Lancaster & Carlisle was at the discussion stage there was bickering about a site for a common station in Carlisle. In fact, the Maryport & Carlisle's Crown Street terminus was sanctioned at the same time as the line from Lancaster. When the Caledonian was authorised in 1845 the impetus for communal facilities gained strength. Initially the four companies agreed on a site in Court Square and an Act for the new station and its approach lines was passed on 27th July 1846. Harmony was short lived however. George Hudson's involvement with Maryport & Carlisle led to the Crown Street saga, as noted earlier, and the Newcastle & Carlisle remained at London Road. Trains from Lancaster and the south, together with those on the partially completed Caledonian line, began to use the embryo Citadel station early in September 1847.

The London & North Western Railway had been formed out of the London & Birmingham, Grand Junction and Liverpool & Manchester on 1st January 1846 and more or less controlled the other companies forming the main line to Lancaster. It also worked the Lancaster & Carlisle from the outset, but terminated the agreement after eleven years leaving the company to run its own trains from August 1857. In September 1859 the old arrangements were reinstated, then on 22nd December 1859 the LNWR leased the Lancaster & Carlisle and finally absorbed it by an Act dated 21st July 1879.

At Carlisle the track layout was modified twice. On 24th January 1862 a new line opened slightly to the west of the original, thus straightening the approach to Citadel from Upperby Junction. This still intersected the North Eastern's Canal branch on the level at St Nicholas Crossing and a serious accident occurred there in the early hours of Sunday 10th July 1870. The 12.48am Midnight Mail had just departed from Carlisle when it was struck in the middle by a North Eastern trip goods from Canal yard driven by the fireman - the driver was still in a local pub. Three coaches were smashed and there were six fatalities. Partly as a result of this collision, but also in association with the new goods avoiding lines, the LNWR tracks were moved slightly to the west again. This elevated deviation opened on 7th July 1877 and crossed the Canal branch by an overbridge.

The main line to Lancaster headed south eastwards from Carlisle in sweeping curves along the west side of the Petteril valley, four miles at 1 in 131 being a trial for up trains. With a former Roman road (now the A6) to the east, the line passed Newbiggin Hall in a cutting and reached 200ft above sea level. At Wreay, 5 miles from Carlisle, the valley

24

Above. **Class 5 No.44929 passes Crown Street goods and the 1951 version of No.5 box, as it approaches Carlisle with the Sunday afternoon Liverpool and Manchester to Glasgow Central service, on 12th July 1964. The twelve coach train was running 40 minutes late and A2 Pacific No.60522 took it forward over Beattock. Photograph W.A.C. Smith.**

Below. **The swansong of steam and the transitional coach livery at Carlisle on 5th August 1967. Black 5 No.44911 climbs away from Citadel with the 11.05 Glasgow - Blackpool. Maryport line on the left, the station itself in the centre background and derelict Crown Street goods on the right. Photograph W.A.C. Smith**

began to close in. Further progress through the Forest of Inglewood, once a great Norman hunting domain, led to Southwaite, 300ft up and 7½ miles from Citadel. At Calthwaite, 10¾ miles from Carlisle and 400ft above the Solway, the River Petteril was bridged. Lazonby Fell then reared up to the east as the line approached Plumpton (13 miles).

At Penrith (17¾ miles) the Lancaster & Carlisle left the red sandstone of the Solway basin behind and entered Pennine limestone country. The town itself grew up in the shadow of a feudal stronghold and developed as an important market centre, but the railway took little heed of medieval heritage and built its station on part of the castle site. A reverse curve took the tracks through the town and across viaducts spanning the River Eamont and River Lowther. Although already 500ft above sea level, trains now faced the real climb - seven miles at 1 in 125 with short stretches of 1 in 106. Great Strickland was passed at 600ft, Little Strickland at 700ft and Sweet Holme at 800ft. By now the landscape was much wilder, with the Lakeland fells prominent to the west.

After Shap station (29¾ miles) the famous 916ft summit was broached, followed by a 60ft deep granite cutting extending for a quarter of a mile. Although a major engineering work, scenically it is rather a disappointment. For the connoisseur of landscape this does not matter that much, for the ensuing descent through the Westmorland fells by way of the Lune gorge is the most impressive part of the West Coast main line, at least in England.

Lancaster & Carlisle stations were designed by Sir William Tite, one of the major names in Victorian railway architecture. He became famous for his work on the London & Southampton railway, but was happy to accept all manner of commissions rather than the occasional prestige job. His smaller creations on the line north of Lancaster were homely Tudor cottages in local stone, wholly in keeping with the fell country. Shap and Plumpton were good examples. Penrith was the largest structure, a sedate Tudor building in local sandstone consisting of a low single-storey range parallel to the platforms relieved by two tall transverse gabled blocks. One of these had a huge mullioned window benevolently peering towards the remains of the castle.

LNWR passenger locos tended to be undersized for their work, a trait maybe inherited from the London & Birmingham Railway with its Bury four-wheelers, but certainly perpetuated by the McConnell 'Bloomers' and Ramsbottom 'Problem' 2-2-2s. These were simple designs from the rival establishments at Wolverton and Crewe, the 'Problem' class being synonymous with the Lancaster & Carlisle line during the 1860s. Webb's 'Jumbo' 2-4-0s proved extremely successful, which is more than could be said for his complicated 2-2-2-0 and 2-2-2-2 'Compounds'. However, in 1895 Webb 4-4-0 'Compound' IONIC hauled a train from Euston to Carlisle without a pause - the longest non-stop run on the LNWR to date. Whale's 'Precursor' 4-4-0s and Bowen Cooke's 'George V' 4-4-0s were also regarded as very good engines, but the former's 'Experiment' 4-6-0s and the latter's 'Prince of Wales' 4-6-0s gained less esteem.

In the early 1900s most LNWR trains arrived at Carlisle double-headed, a Webb 'Compound' and 'Jumbo' pilot being a typical combination. Nevertheless, some expresses were entrusted to a solitary 'Precursor' or 'Experiment'. In either case they were an impressive sight, the locomotives in fully lined-out 'blackberry' black and the coaches sporting a regal plum and 'spilt milk' livery. Even the LNWR's first really big passenger engines, the 'Claughton' 4-6-0s of 1913 had relatively small boilers, although some of them were rebuilt with larger ones in early LMS days. By 1923 'Prince of Wales' 4-6-2Ts were a familiar sight on the main line to Penrith and Lancaster, while 'DX' and 'Cauliflower' 0-6-0s and Bowen Cooke 0-8-0s handled freight traffic into Carlisle.

The Lancaster & Carlisle section of the LNWR was dominated by long distance main line services, with local passenger trains very much a secondary consideration. As is well known, of course, expresses became national news in the races to Scotland during late Victorian times. The 1888 races to Edinburgh saw the 90 miles from Preston to Carlisle covered in 89 minutes, as opposed to the nor-

25

mal 105 minutes, whilst on the final night of the 1895 races to Aberdeen a huge crowd gathered at Citadel around 12.30am to watch the West Coast train arrive. It had left Euston just 4hrs 36mins earlier, with HARDWICKE in charge since Crewe.

In the decade leading up to World War I Citadel dealt with around sixty LNWR trains on weekdays, of which over forty were expresses. An interesting feature was the number of overnight trains which called between 1am and 6am. This nocturnal operation reached epic proportions during the build up to the beginning of grouse shooting in August - the glorious 12th. As many as 300 beds would be made up in 1st class sleeping cars at Euston on August 10th and LNWR coaches ventured far into the Highlands. In 1905 the overnight departures from Carlisle were as follows, destinations of through carriages being shown in brackets :
1.12am (Perth, Aberdeen,
Dava, Lochalsh);
1.35am (Inverness, Altnabreac);
1.45am (Aberdeen)
2.08am (Aberdeen)
2.18am (Oban, Aberdeen, Alford);
2.22am (Aberdeen, The Mound);
2.39am (Stranraer);
3.15am (Edinburgh, Glasgow);
3.35am (Edinburgh, Glasgow -
ex Birmingham);
3.45am (Glasgow - ex Exeter);
3.55am (Glasgow, Gourock);
4.15am (Perth)

When the LMS took over in 1923 the normal weekday pattern on the West Coast main line consisted of three up expresses to Euston and two down workings to Glasgow and Edinburgh between noon and 2pm, a second identical group between 3.45pm and 5.45pm, and four up sleepers balanced by the same number of down sleepers between midnight and 7am. In addition there were fast trains from Liverpool/Manchester and Birmingham to Glasgow/Edinburgh and vice versa. Initially, ex-LNWR locos reigned supreme, but the next decade and a half saw a revolution in motive power. First to arrive were the Hughes/Fowler 4-6-0s and 'Crab' 2-6-0s inspired by the former Lancashire & Yorkshire Railway, followed by the 'Royal Scot' and 'Patriot' 4-6-0s.

After a slightly shaky start, matters improved dramatically with the arrival of Stanier from Swindon. His taper boiler 'Princess Royal' Pacifics were introduced in 1933 and the 'Princess Coronation' 4-6-2s soon followed. Most of the latter appeared as streamliners and became celebrities when they worked the prestigious 'Coronation Scot' Euston - Glasgow express from 1937. Stanier's 'Jubilee' 4-6-0s and ubiquitous mixed traffic 4-6-0s (the Black 5s) were both introduced in 1934 and provided further variety to the

Top. Class 5 4-6-0 No.45339 passes a still busy Upperby yard and approaches Citadel station with a down parcels train, on 6th April 1963. The carriage sidings and engine shed can be seen in the background. Photograph W.A.C. Smith.

Middle. Britannia Pacific No.70032 TENNYSON storms past Upperby with the 14.00 from Glasgow Central to Liverpool and Manchester on 12th August 1967. Maroon stock is interspersed with 'corporate image' blue and grey. Photograph W.A.C. Smith.

Bottom. A thunderstorm rages as passenger and goods trains make simultaneous departures from Carlisle on 12th August 1967. 5MT 4-6-0 No.45038 passes Upperby Bridge Junction (No.13) signal box with the 11.05 Glasgow - Blackpool as another Black 5 waits to get the Larbert soda ash working on the move. Photograph W.A.C. Smith.

daily diet at Citadel. Following nationalisation new 'Clan' Pacifics worked certain trains to Glasgow and Manchester, whilst the standard types such as 'Britannia' Pacifics and 9F 2-10-0s appeared in due course.

From the late 1940s local passenger workings from Carlisle to Penrith and Keswick were hauled by Ivatt class 2 moguls or even an old LNWR 'Cauliflower' 0-6-0, but there was little traffic on offer at intermediate Lancaster & Carlisle stations. Wreay had already closed on 16th August 1943 and Plumpton followed on 31st May 1948. Southwaite and Calthwaite were denied services from 7th April 1952, leaving the main line south free for expresses. Meanwhile, diesels had appeared in the form of 10000 and 10001, Co-Co machines built by English Electric in 1947. Steam nevertheless reigned supreme until 1961 when English Electric Type 4s (class 40) began to take over principal West Coast expresses. At the time, services over the Lancaster & Carlisle followed the traditional pattern, with overnight sleepers and daytime workings to Euston, Manchester and Birmingham.

Brush Type 4 diesels (class 47) were employed on expresses from 1967 and pairs of English Electric class 50 diesels became the norm in 1970. At the time the line to Lancaster and the south saw very little goods traffic apart from freightliners and parcels - most of it went via the Settle & Carlisle route. Electrification from Weaver Junction to Glasgow was authorised in 1970 at an estimated cost of £75 million and regular traffic 'under the wires' began on 6th May 1974. In 1997, class 86, 87 and 90 electric locos working push-pull sets provide Euston and Birmingham New Street services, eleven of which run on normal weekdays. South Coast and West Country services to Brighton, Bournemouth, Poole, Plymouth and Penzance consist mainly of Intercity 125s. An train even runs to London Paddington, which no doubt would have astonished the LNWR. Class 158s provide through workings to Manchester Airport and Liverpool. Two overnight trains, the 'Caledonian Sleepers', serve Glasgow/Edinburgh and Aberdeen/Inverness/Fort William respectively. Eurostars from Paris and Brussels are scheduled to start shortly.

Britannia Pacific No.70051 FIRTH OF FORTH of Crewe North shed approaches Shap summit with a Manchester Victoria - Glasgow Central express, on Saturday 29th August 1963. Photograph G.W. Morrison.

Over a century after the Lancaster & Carlisle was built, the brooding Westmorland fells still seemed to resent the presence of a railway. Preston 2P 4-4-0 No.40694 and Polmadie Britannia Pacific No.70054 DORNOCH FIRTH struggle to lift a seventeen coach Manchester - Glasgow train up to Shap summit on 26th May 1958. Photograph G.W. Morrison.

Above. Caledonian super-power heading for Beattock. McIntosh superheated '179' class 4-6-0 No.180 leaves Carlisle with a mixed goods around 1920. Just seven years old and still resplendent in Caley blue, the engine was one of eleven built for express goods traffic. They were unusual for the Caledonian in having side-window cabs. Photograph J.F. Ward Collection.

Below. The Caley main line and its former LNWR counterpart continued to share the cream of LMS motive power in 1937. Stanier streamlined Coronation Pacific No.6227 DUCHESS OF DEVONSHIRE leaves Carlisle in bright sunshine with the down Euston - Glasgow 'Royal Scot'. Photograph Neville Stead Collection.

Chapter 5
CALEDONIAN

Although the Caledonian eventually became the aristocrat of Scottish railways, its conception and early finances had English roots. Construction work on the London & Birmingham and Grand Junction was still underway when the latter instructed its engineer Joseph Locke to survey a route from Preston to the Clyde valley. North of Carlisle he liked the look of Annandale, but was put off by the mountain barrier north of Moffat and recommended an easier course through Nithsdale, albeit a less direct one. James Hope-Johnstone, MP and proprietor of the Annandale estates, was aware of the potential benefits of railways and asked Locke to examine the route to Glasgow again. The engineer concurred and decided that a line through the hills west of Moffat was feasible, despite the gradients.

This initial activity was back in 1837, but the prospect of a lengthy railway through lonely countryside attracted virtually no promise of cash from Scotland. Even the English proprietors who had suggested the line were too busy with other schemes to think about matters north of Carlisle. However, these were heady days for the new form of transport and by 1840 the campaign to link the existing networks either side of the Border had become frantic. The Annandale/Nithsdale debate emerged again and there were hints of a main line from York to Edinburgh via Newcastle. In March 1841 the government commission decided that only one route was necessary and this should be along Annandale. It was also emphasised that in the national interest, the line should be built quickly.

Rather than settling the issue, the report actually stimulated competition. One outcome was the National Railway of Scotland which intended to build a line from Lancaster to Edinburgh via Carlisle and Peebles for £4 million, but it slid into oblivion as the Annandale scheme gathered strength. The latter project was getting underway by the end of 1841, although progress proved sluggish. In fact it was not until 1844 that active promotion commenced and the name 'Caledonian Railway' emerged. Despite being funded mainly from England, the first route from Carlisle to the north was proudly Scottish and described itself as the 'National Line'.

In a scene which could have been straight out of 'Just William' a youthful spotter with a box camera captures No.46242 CITY OF GLASGOW at close quarters. The Camden Pacific is taking water at Citadel during its trek south with the up 'Caledonian' in August 1959. Photograph W.A.C. Smith.

Rebuilt Royal Scot 4-6-0 No.46110 GRENADIER GUARDSMAN rolls into Citadel on 25th September 1961 with the 10.50am from Glasgow Central to Liverpool Exchange and Manchester Victoria. Victoria Road viaduct in the background was built in 1877 to connect the centre of Carlisle with suburban development on the west side of the city. Photograph W.A.C. Smith.

The Caledonian Railway acquired its Act of Parliament on 31st July 1845 and at 122 miles was one of the largest projects sanctioned thus far. From Carlisle the line was to head northwards up Annandale to a summit at Beattock in the Lowther Hills before descending towards the Clyde valley. Access to Glasgow would be via local lines which needed regauging and upgrading. At Carstairs another line would strike across the moors to Edinburgh. The Caledonian came into being at an exciting time, in the full flow of the 'Railway Mania', and lines to Perth, Dundee and Aberdeen were authorised at the same time. A couple of decades later these were absorbed by the Caledonian, largely justifying the self-proclaimed 'National Line' status.

Joseph Locke was appointed engineer. A practical, far-seeing man, he was a master of organisation and made sure that his lines were built properly. Thomas Brassey was the contractor and he was capable of organising works on a massive scale. At the peak of activity, 20,000 men were employed along the length of the route. Thomas Carlyle, the historian, gave his own view of the scene at his birthplace, Ecclefechan:

'The country is greatly in a state of derangement. The harvest, with its black potato fields, no great things, and all roads and lanes overrun with drunken navvies; for our great Caledonian Railway passes in this direction, and all the world here, as everywhere, calculates on getting to Heaven by steam! I have not in my travels seen anything uglier than that disorganic mass of labourers, sunk three-fold deeper in brutality by the three-fold wages they are getting. The Yorkshire and Lancashire men, I hear, are reckoned the worst; and not without glad surprise, I find the Irish are the best in point of behaviour. The English, who eat twice as much beef, consume the residue in whisky.'

The southern section of the Caledonian, from the new joint station at Carlisle to Beattock deep in the Southern Uplands, opened on 10th September 1847. On 15th February 1848 through services to Glasgow and Edinburgh commenced. Success was immediate. On 10th March 1848 the Post Office transferred its business from the East Coast route and two through services commenced; the 'Day Mail' leaving Euston at 8.30am and the 'Night Mail' departing at 8.45pm. On 1st May 1848 the first regular express passenger trains began to run from Euston to Glasgow and Edinburgh. For the first time it was possible to travel from London to Scotland by rail without a change of carriage. At the same time, through services to Liverpool, Manchester and Birmingham began to run over Caledonian metals. On 26th June 1848 livestock trains to England were inaugurated and they became over-subscribed within days. Also lucrative, but decidedly unofficial, was the traffic in a certain liquid. Until 1850 the duty on whisky was less in Scotland than in England, so many a Caledonian tender concealed bottles of the potent amber fluid as trains crossed the Border!

Despite the government commission's recommendation nine years earlier, there were three Anglo-Scottish routes by 1850, both the North British and Glasgow & South Western providing fierce competition. Meanwhile, Caledonian affairs had become a shambles despite the burgeoning traffic. From the outset the company had been over ambitious and even tried to lease the Newcastle & Carlisle in 1848 to gain access to the East Coast route. The financial situation was desperate in 1849 and the directors asked the LNWR to work its system - a request turned down flat by Euston. In February 1850 a thorough investigation was launched into the structure and operations of the Caledonian.

As a result, the ruinous competition between Glasgow and Edinburgh was

Stanier class 5 4-6-0 No.45013 passes Caldew Bridge and slows for the approach to Citadel with the 10.10am Edinburgh Princes Street - Birmingham New Street on 28th September 1963. Caldew Junction (Carlisle No.3) signal box in the background, the goods avoiding lines on the left and the abandoned approach to Viaduct yard in the foreground. Photograph W.A.C. Smith.

An Illustrated History of Carlisle's Railways

Britannia Pacific No.70041 SIR JOHN MOORE gathers speed as its heads north past Port Carlisle Junction with the 9.25am Crewe - Perth on 8th May 1965. Caldew Junction box (seen above the rear of the train) controlled the divergence of the Waverley route tracks, veering off in the right foreground. Photograph W.A.C. Smith

halted, excess staff were dismissed, pay cuts were implemented, directors' expenses were virtually abolished and close scrutiny was exercised over day to day procedures. From the brink of catastrophe the company began a steady climb to prosperity and eventually pre-eminence. In conjunction with the LNWR, the stranglehold on West Coast traffic was tightened. Glasgow Central opened during 1879, providing a far more convenient terminus in Scotland's largest city. In 1885 two Travelling Post Office trains were introduced from Euston to Glasgow, the Caledonian 'Day Down' and LNWR 'Night Down'.

Along with the LNWR climb to Shap, the Caledonian ascent to Beattock became one of the classic stretches of main line for train recorders and photographers. Heading north out of Carlisle, trains first run past the cathedral, West Walls and castle before crossing the River Caldew on a skew bridge. An embankment across parkland leads to the River Eden bridge at Etterby, followed by a level stretch past Kingmoor. Stations were provided for the village of Rockcliffe (4 miles from Citadel) and remote farmland at Floriston (6 miles). Shortly afterwards a viaduct crosses the tidal River Esk, flat ground then leading to Gretna station (8½ miles). Another bridge spans the River Sark which marks the England/Scotland border at this point. Here the line is still only about 50ft above sea level, but a westerly course soon lifts the track up to Kirkpatrick (13 miles). More earthworks become evident as the railway climbs up the wooded Kirtle Water valley to Kirtlebridge (16 miles) where the Solway lowlands give way to the Southern Upland foothills. Ecclefechan (19 miles) is followed by a sweeping reverse curve past the Castlemilk estate, reaching a 320ft summit in a substantial cutting, roughly mid-way.

Progress northwards is generally downhill for a while, beginning with a viaduct over Water of Milk. By Dryfe Water, just beyond Lockerbie (26 miles) the tracks have descended to 210ft. Lockerbie itself became famous for sheep sales, notably the great Autumn Lamb Fair. The climb resumes, moderately at first, along the eastern side of the River Annan valley. At Wamphray the tracks switch to the west bank and continue to Beattock (330ft above sea level and 40 miles from Carlisle). For the next 10 miles the ascent is punishing.

The River Annan tumbles down from 2,651 ft Hart Fell above Moffat, the sheer wall of the Devil's Beef Tub preventing any railway progress in this direction. Instead, the track climbs relentlessly at 1 in 88, then 1 in 74 alongside Evan Water. At Harthope, where a bridge spans the main Carlisle - Glasgow road, the altitude is 820ft. Eventually, deep in the Lowther Hills, the famous 1,016ft Beattock summit is breasted fifty miles from Citadel. Ahead lies the descent to Carstairs, Motherwell and Glasgow.

Intermediate stations on the Caledonian main line were often quite harsh, but in keeping with the hills and local architectural traditions. Walls were a mixture of rough-hewn stone and large dressed blocks, whilst the windows and doors usually had substantial yet plain casements. There was a moderately steep pitch to the roofs and gable ends were crow-stepped, as at Lockerbie, or plain with a single step as at Wamphray. Tall, square chimneys with a broader top formed a distinctive feature.

Three branches diverged from the Caledonian in the southern Borders. first came the Dumfries, Lochmaben & Lockerbie Railway, a Caledonian subsidiary and a deliberate thrust into Glasgow & South Western territory. This 14½ mile route past Castle Loch and round the northern slopes of Hightown Hill opened on 1st September 1863 using a bay platform at Dumfries rather than a separate terminus as originally envisaged. The Caledonian introduced a through Dumfries - Edinburgh service, which was soon countered by a similar G&SW working via Gretna and the North British Waverley route. A few miles further north was the

Rebuilt Patriot 4-6-0 No.45512 BUNSEN crosses the River Eden at Etterby with the Sunday morning Liverpool and Manchester train for Glasgow Central on 12th July 1964. This comprised fourteen vehicles and was running 20 minutes late. The bridge for the goods lines on the right was built in 1942 as a wartime measure. Note Carlisle's castle and cathedral in the distance. Photograph W.A.C. Smith.

Moffat Railway, a locally promoted 1¾ mile branch from Beattock, opened on 2nd April 1883 to serve the flourishing spa town.

The third branch was a remarkable affair, and undoubtedly the most spectacular stretch of track across the actual England/Scotland border. With some 100,000 tons of Cumbrian hematite ore consumed by Lanarkshire iron furnaces during 1863, there was considerable impetus for a direct line avoiding the detour via Carlisle. This, of course, meant crossing the Solway estuary at some point. With a lot of Caledonian money behind it, the Solway Junction Railway was authorised on 30th June 1864 and construction of the 21¼ mile route from Kirtlebridge to Brayton on the Maryport & Carlisle commenced the following March.

From Kirtlebridge a series of sweeping curves through hilly ground east of the River Annan brought the railway to Annan itself. The line then headed directly for the shore and crossed the Solway on a metal viaduct extending for no less than 1,950 yds - the longest in the world at the time. Most of this frail-looking structure consisted of a wrought iron deck resting on 193 piers, each of which comprised groups of one-foot diameter cast iron columns. The remainder of the route ran across virtually level ground, utilising the North British Silloth branch between Kirkbride and Abbeyholme.

Goods traffic began on 13th September 1869 and a passenger service from Kirtlebridge to Brayton commenced on 8th August 1870, through trains taking nearly an hour. Initially the line carried its fair share of minerals, but by the mid-1870s imported Spanish ore had virtually put paid to the West Cumberland trade. In winter 1881 ice floes demolished

Top. The down side of Kirtlebridge station from the 1.50pm Glasgow Central - Carlisle, hauled by Patricroft Jubilee No.45663 JERVIS on 23rd May 1960. Solway Junction trains to Brayton on the Maryport & Carlisle line via Solway Viaduct commenced from the far side of the island platform. Photograph W.A.C. Smith.

Middle. Ex-Caledonian Lambie 4-4-0T No.15027 stands at Annan Shawhill with a mixed train from Kirtlebridge, shortly before this remnant of the Solway Junction Railway closed to passenger traffic in April 1931. The crew and station staff have been joined by the local newspaper delivery boy for this commemorative photograph. Photograph J.J. Cunningham.

Bottom. Ecclefechan signal box, south of Lockerbie, on 5th June 1968, with the photographer's Rolls Royce Silver Cloud in the background. It may come as a surprise that some main line cabins were this small. The box closed at the end of 1971, a victim of resignalling prior to electrification. Photograph F.W. Shuttleworth.

Black 5 4-6-0 No.45061 heads north through Lockerbie with a train of sheeted wagons on 25th February 1967. The course of the Dumfries branch curves right in the foreground whilst the disused engine shed is on the left. This survived for another twenty years or so. Photograph W.A.C. Smith.

45 of the piers and the viaduct remained closed for three years. During 1893 the Caledonian absorbed what was, to quote John Thomas, 'a moribund international branch'.

The first Caledonian passenger engines were Crewe-type 2-2-2s, goods traffic being handled by 0-4-2s. By the mid-1850s a larger 7ft 2in single-driver design by Sinclair was in service and these were followed by Connor 'eight-footers' which regularly worked between Glasgow and Carlisle, along with some 7ft 2-4-0s, until the arrival of Drummond's 4-4-0s in 1884. Meanwhile, the first of a large fleet of 0-6-0 goods locos, popularly known as 'Jumbos' had entered service.

Timing was tight on the main line, as demonstrated by an incident in 1892. Gladstone, on one of his 'whistle-stop' tours made political speeches at stations; at Lockerbie the welcome was so verbose that the train had to leave before the great man had time to address the assembled throng. Speed became an obsession during the 1880s and 1890s with the 'races' to Edinburgh and Aberdeen. One of the stars was 4-2-2 No.123 with its dash over Beattock at an average of nearly 60mph. At the turn of the century, after the excitement had died down, some 45 Caledonian trains were dealt with at Citadel on normal weekdays, ten of them commencing or terminating at the Border City.

The first of the celebrated McIntosh 'Dunalastair' 4-4-0s appeared in 1896 and the breed culminated in the '140' class of 1904. Pickersgill's variant was built from 1916. In 1903 two huge 4-6-0s emerged from St Rollox works and three years later they were followed by the famous 'Cardean' class. For ten years No 903 regularly worked the 2pm 'Corridor' out of Glasgow and the 8.13pm return working from Carlisle. Express goods '918' and '179' 4-6-0s also appeared on the main line, together with eight 0-8-0s for mineral traffic.

Beattock presented an even greater challenge when heavy passenger trains became the norm, the ubiquitous and long-lived McIntosh 0-4-4Ts providing banking assistance for many years. Pickersgill's big 4-6-2Ts were tried briefly as well. Although class '60' 4-6-0s continued to plod over the summit until early BR years, the large McIntosh 4-6-0s never seemed to recover from World War 1 and by the grouping of 1923 Caledonian main line passenger trains were monopolised by pairs of 4-4-0s. They were soon joined by standard LMS Compound 4-4-0s which were regarded with suspicion by Scottish men at first. Eventually they became accepted and saw regular use well into the 1950s. Then came the 'Royal Scot', 'Jubilee' and 'Black 5' 4-6-0s, pending the introduction of Stanier's magnificent 'Duchess' Pacifics which admirably upheld the Caley's slogan 'The True to Time Line'.

Numerous Caledonian Engines lasted well into nationalisation, notably the later 0-4-4Ts and 'Jumbo' 0-6-0s, together with McIntosh and Pickersgill 4-4-0s relegated to lighter duties. BR Standard classes such as 'Clan' and 'Britannia' Pacifics appeared, whilst No 71000 DUKE OF GLOUCESTER was a regular performer on the 'Mid-day Scot'. Nevertheless, the 'Coronations' remained the mainstay of principal services over Beattock, until displaced by English Electric Type 4 diesels in 1961.

A century and a half after it was built, the former Caledonian main line is as important as ever, but over the last 75 years it has gradually been stripped of its branches and wayside stations. As early as 1914 the ailing Solway viaduct had a 10mph speed restriction imposed on it, although World War 1 saw a marked increase in traffic as a result of the demand for pig iron by armaments factories. This proved a temporary reprieve, for the solitary return passenger service (a mixed train) between Annan and Brayton was withdrawn by the Caledonian on 20th May 1921. Goods traffic ceased three months later on 30th August and the viaduct was demolished over a twenty month period in 1934-35. Passenger trains from Kirtlebridge to Annan Shaw Hill (still six a day in the 1920s) continued until 27th April 1931 and the line was used for goods traffic for another eight years.

During 1942 a second two-track viaduct was built where the main line crossed the River Eden just north of Carlisle. This was a strategic measure in view of possible bomb damage. Shortly after

An Illustrated History of Carlisle's Railways

Left. A solitary passenger strides down the rainswept platform at Wamphray having left the afternoon up 'Parly' (1.50pm all stations Glasgow Central - Carlisle) on 23rd May 1960, three weeks before wayside stations between Carlisle and Beattock closed. The building is a fine example of the rugged architectural style adopted by the Caledonian in the late 1840s. Photograph W.A.C. Smith.

Below. Fowler 2-6-4T No.42320 from Upperby shed was an unusual sight banking at Beattock on 29th July 1961. Although five out of the seven tanks based at Beattock for assisting main line trains were in use, further help was clearly needed on this busy Saturday. This service is the 9.15am Liverpool Exchange - Glasgow Central consisting of twelve coaches double headed by a pair of 'Black 5s' and running 32 minutes late. The Moffat branch is visible just above the banker. Photograph W.A.C. Smith.

nationalisation, retrenchment resumed with the closure of Rockcliffe and Floriston to all traffic on 17th July 1950, Gretna following suit on 10th September 1951. The branch from Lockerbie to Dumfries lost its passenger trains on 19th May 1952 and Beattock - Moffat services ceased on 6th December 1954. Then there was a lull, but six intermediate stations south of Beattock - including Wamphray, Ecclefechan, Kirtlebridge and Kirkpatrick - passed into oblivion on 13th June 1960.

Beeching had little effect, apart from precipitating the end of the branch goods service to Moffat on 6th April 1964. Somewhat belatedly, Beattock station expired on 3rd January 1972. Electrification of the former Caledonian main line was inaugurated on 6th May 1974 and the usually smooth West Coast operation north of Carlisle now pays little heed to Border communities, with the exception of Lockerbie.

Below. Fairburn 2-6-4T No.42688 simmers in summer sunshine at Beattock summit as it waits for a path back to Beattock station, having banked English Electric type 4 No.D333 on the 14-coach down 'Royal Scot'. The date is 29th July 1961. Photograph W.A.C. Smith.

Right. An idyllic branch line scene at Moffat on 4th December 1954, the last day of passenger services. The delightful 1883 terminus was host to ex-Caledonian Pickersgill 0-4-4T No.55232 with a solitary coach waiting to leave at 3.05pm for the 5 minute journey to Beattock. Although propelling from Moffat was the norm, none of the Beattock engines had push/pull equipment! Some 15 runs each way were made daily, except Sunday, one of them being designated 'mixed'. Photograph W.A.C. Smith.

Top. Manson 4-6-0 No.385 in magnificent repose at Citadel in 1906. The engine was built in 1903 but suffered premature withdrawal as No.14660 in 1927 - a victim of the wholesale slaughter of G&SW motive power ordered by the LMS. Photograph J.F. Ward Collection.

Below. Having backed down from Kingmoor shed, Black 5 No.44887 stands in the centre road at Citadel ready to take over 1S52, the 06.40 Birmingham - Glasgow which arrived behind 'Jubilee' No.45562. The diesel in this 19th August 1967 view was waiting to haul the 09.25 from Blackpool forward to Glasgow. Photograph W.A.C. Smith.

Chapter 6
GLASGOW & SOUTH WESTERN

Of the three Scottish railway companies serving Carlisle, the Glasgow & South Western had the most notable ancestry. One of the lines which eventually became part of its system was the Kilmarnock & Troon, Scotland's earliest passenger line and the first in that country to try steam locomotives (in 1816-17). Nevertheless, the 'Sou' West' was a poor relation at Citadel for many years, despite reaching the Border City just after the Caledonian. Matters improved considerably following the opening of the Midland's Settle & Carlisle route which provided an independent outlet to the south. The G&SW built up a stud of distinctive engines, but along with those belonging to the Maryport & Carlisle most were swiftly eliminated as the LMS pursued standardisation.

The story of the line from Glasgow to Kilmarnock, Dumfries and Carlisle began in 1836 when Joseph Locke was surveying the route through the Southern Uplands on behalf of the Grand Junction Railway. When the engineer decided that the climb beyond Moffat at the head of Annandale was too steep he returned to Gretna and examined the easier Nithsdale passage. Although the mileage between Carlisle and Glasgow would have been greater, there were two advantages. Firstly, the line would serve Dumfries and Kilmarnock, both of which were important manufacturing and market towns. Secondly, the Glasgow, Paisley, Kilmarnock and Ayr Railway was at the planning stage and would provide an ideal springing point for the trunk route to England.

The subsequent pressure on Locke to examine the Annandale route again has been outlined in the Caledonian chapter. When his new survey was published in 1837 the Glasgow, Paisley, Kilmarnock & Ayr had been authorised and there was confident talk of a triangle of railways linking Glasgow, Carlisle and Portpatrick on the Irish Sea coast. When the Annandale line received government blessing only one Anglo-Scottish route was envisaged. The Glasgow promoters were far from pleased; they had intended to finance the Nithsdale project themselves and felt betrayed by Locke and his English masters.

DUMFRIES

Trains began running from Glasgow to Ayr in 1840 and the line proved a great success. A steamer service from Ardrossan to Liverpool was also inaugurated, but this particular venture did not live up to expectations. The Ayrshire company therefore turned its attention to finding a rail route to England, the Dalry - Kilmarnock branch (opened in 1843) being an unmistakable finger pointing towards Carlisle. Shortly afterwards the Glasgow, Dumfries & Carlisle Railway was formed and immediately found itself in the thick of the Nithsdale/Annandale debate. There was an agreement whereby the Kilmarnock branch would be extended

On 22nd July 1967 English Electric Type 3 No.D6852 comes off the 13.25 from Glasgow to Morecambe which had reached Carlisle via Dumfries. As rostered, it is replaced by steam traction in the form of Black 5 4-6-0 No.45072. Photograph W.A.C. Smith.

G&SW Smellie 4-4-0 No.458 passing Rockcliffe on the Caledonian main line with a short freight composed mainly of cattle wagons. The engine was withdrawn in 1926 as LMS No.14151.

to Cumnock to meet the Dumfries line, thus creating a new trunk route. Naturally, the embryo Caledonian was totally against this proposal.

Bills for the Glasgow, Paisley, Kilmarnock & Ayr extension and the Glasgow, Dumfries & Carlisle were presented to parliament in 1845. The former was authorised on 28th July of that year, but the latter failed in the face of vehement Caledonian objections. A revised Dumfries scheme, this time stemming from the Caley at Gretna, received its Act on 16th July 1846. Gradually the new lines crept towards each other. Kilmarnock trains continued to Auchinleck from 9th August 1848 and the Auchinleck - New Cumnock section opened on 20th May 1850. The Gretna - Dumfries tracks began to carry traffic on 23rd August 1848, the extension to Closeburn following on 15th October 1849. Eventually the difficult Closeburn - New Cumnock gap was closed on 28th October 1850 and through services between Glasgow and Gretna commenced. On the same day the Ayrshire and Dumfries companies amalgamated to form the Glasgow & South Western Railway.

Although the G&SW was admitted to Citadel on 1st March 1851 and shared the Caledonian goods yard and engine shed at West Walls, the two companies remained bitter rivals. The newcomer was truly Scottish and regarded the Annandale company as a puppet of the LNWR. For its part, the Caledonian made matters as difficult as possible, charging £5,000 per annum for the use of its tracks south of Gretna Junction and a further £1,000 for access to Citadel. Needless to say, relations at West Walls were uneasy as well. In 1852 the Sou'West drew up a bill for an independent line from Gretna to Brampton on the Newcastle & Carlisle, but this was thrown out of parliament.

The G&SW made no attempt to compete with the Caley for through Glasgow - Carlisle traffic. During the 1850s timings over the Nithsdale route were approaching $4^{3}/_{4}$ hours, as opposed to $3^{1}/_{4}$ hours via Beattock. However, the South Western did find itself involved in a unique aspect of the passenger business - the notorious 'anvil marriages' at Gretna Green increased markedly once the railway opened! More important from the strategic point of view was the completion in 1873 of a line from Kilmarnock to Barrhead which cut several miles off the approach to Glasgow.

Frustration over the lack of an independent outlet to the south led the G&SW to express unbounded support for the Midland's Settle & Carlisle proposal during the early 1860s. After a decade of anticipation, the long-awaited link to Yorkshire, the Midlands and London opened in 1876. St Enoch terminus in Glasgow was completed at the same time, providing superb facilities in the centre of the city. A mutually beneficial partnership between the G&SW and Midland blossomed immediately, the former proudly taking over through coaches from St Pancras for the climb up Nithsdale. By this time Citadel had virtually taken on the mantle of a frontier station, akin to those in Europe.

At first there were few sidings in Carlisle where goods wagons could be exchanged, so shunting took place at Gretna - even on the Sabbath. This angered the local clergy so much that a wordy missive was sent to the General Assembly of the Church of Scotland in Edinburgh urging them to 'suppress the evil'. The G&SW agreed to undertake Sunday shunting, amongst the Godless English at Carlisle, as soon as yards became available.

Exchanges of a different kind - those involving expresses from St Pancras to St Enoch - took place at Citadel. For fourteen years Midland trains were split into Edinburgh and Glasgow portions at Carlisle, a North British loco taking the front coaches forward to Waverley and a South Western engine hauling the remainder to Dumfries, where a second 4-4-0 was attached for the climb through the Lowther Hills. Loadings increased to such an extent that separate trains became the norm from 1890.

The Nithsdale route left the Caledonian at Gretna Junction, nine miles from Citadel and immediately north of the Border. A sharp curve to the west led to Gretna Green station ($9^{3}/_{4}$ miles from Carlisle), followed by an easy run to Annan along the coastal plain, largely within a couple of miles of the Solway shore. Intermediate stations were provided at Rigg

Class 5MT 4-6-0 No.45138 calls at dilapidated Eastriggs station on 15th August 1964 with the 6.10pm Carlisle - Glasgow St. Enoch. Apart from the photographer, the only customer was a railwayman with haversack and bicycle. The building at Eastriggs survives as a house. Photograph W.A.C. Smith.

An Illustrated History of Carlisle's Railways

On the dismal afternoon of 15th August 1964, A1 No.60134 FOXHUNTER calls at Annan with the 2.00pm Glasgow St. Enoch - Carlisle local. Apart from the use of Sprinters on the Sou'West route and the reduction of the goods loop to a siding, the scene is little changed today. The fine G&SW building, which retains its canopy, is now the Station Restaurant. Photograph W.A.C. Smith.

(11½ miles) and Dornock (14¾ miles). Just beyond Annan (17¾ miles) a low viaduct crossed the tidal River Annan, then the railway headed almost due west to Cummertrees (22 miles) where it turned north westwards towards Ruthwell. Even today this is lonely countryside typified by hamlets, isolated farms and patches of woodland.

After Ruthwell (26 miles), Panteth Hill encroached on the perfectly straight formation, forcing the rails to climb to 130ft above sea level in a cutting. At Racks (30 miles), desolate Craigs Moss stretched away to the south west, beyond which the bulk of 1,867ft Criffel dominated the skyline. A pronounced curve to the north brought the G&SW into Dumfries, one of the major goals of the line. Thus far, trains had travelled 33½ miles from Citadel - and Nithsdale beckoned.

The railway crossed the River Nith a mile north of Dumfries station and kept to the west side of the valley for a while, passing Hollywood on the way. Another bridge near Portrack led the line to the eastern side of Nithsdale where it stayed for over 35 miles, to the headwaters and the summit of the route. The terrain became increasingly rugged and beautiful, but demanded numerous earthworks and curves past Auldgirth, Closeburn and Thornhill to maintain a course suitable for expresses. After Carronbridge the track ventured up the Carron Water valley for a couple of miles then plunged through a ridge by means of Drumlanrig tunnel, thereby keeping the line out of sight of Drumlanrig Castle.

Nithsdale was regained at Enterkinfoot and a gorge-like section below the lower slopes of 2,379ft Lowther Hill took the line to Sanquhar, just under sixty miles from Carlisle. The rails were now almost 500ft above sea level, but at least the valley broadened out, giving an easier passage to Kirkconnel, New Cumnock and Polquhap summit at about 600ft. Ahead lay Cumnock, the Ayrshire coalfield, Kilmarnock and Glasgow.

The G&SW adopted a fairly modest approach when it came to station architecture. In the Solway lowlands, local red sandstone was employed and the buildings were substantial enough, but ornamentation was kept to the minimum. Common features included very low-pitched roofs and stubby chimneys, sometimes finished off decoratively at the top. Plain cottages sufficed at smaller places such as Dornock, whilst a two-storey structure with a cross gable and prominent overhanging eaves was provided at Annan. Dumfries also enjoyed the services of a large two-storey building, featuring dormer windows and plain bargeboards. Here, the platforms were on a curve and very attractive canopies provided shelter.

Dumfries eventually became an important junction where the 'Port Road' to Stranraer, together with a pair of branches to Lockerbie and Moniaive respectively, left the G&SW main line. The first resulted from the lure of the short sea crossing from Portpatrick to Ireland. This passage had been established by carts and sailing ships centuries earlier, but new facilities at harbours such as Holyhead and Fleetwood had rendered it moribund. The Lockerbie line involved territory and tactics; it has been described in the Caledonian chapter. Finally, the Moniaive branch was a latecomer which tapped a remote rural area.

The Castle Douglas & Dumfries Railway opened on 7th November 1859. Although leaving the Glasgow line half a mile north of Dumfries station, the branch immediately turned south westwards and climbed towards a gap in the Criffel massif about 300ft above sea level. A descent past Beeswing led to Dalbeattie, followed by a twisting course through hilly country to Castle Douglas. The straggling extension to the Irish Sea was built by the Portpatrick Railway, opened as far as Stranraer on 12th March 1861 and Portpatrick eighteen months later. It passed through wild country, encountering moorland, peat bogs and lochs, together with several deep valleys which had to be spanned by viaducts.

A rose, thistle and shamrock adorned the seal of the Portpatrick Railway, emphasising its international nature.

Wet summer weather, 15th August 1964, and A1 4-6-2 No.60131 OSPREY approaches Annan with the 9.30am summer relief from London St. Pancras to Glasgow St. Enoch. Solway ground frame, to the right of the engine, gave access to an engineering works at the time, but the siding was once a spur connecting with the Solway Junction line from Kirtlebridge to Brayton. Photograph W.A.C. Smith.

Locally shedded class 5 4-6-0 No.45169, in immaculate condition, awaits departure from Dumfries with an up parcels train on 13th June 1959. Although the centre road has been removed, the up side platform canopy shortened, and the north end down side bays infilled, the station remains an attractive reminder of bygone days. Photograph W.A.C. Smith.

Although the G&SW was expected to work the line, the Caledonian came up with a better deal and ran trains through Galloway for over twenty years. Despite carrying plenty of Irish traffic, the Portpatrick company got into dire straits and had to be bailed out in 1885 by the formation of the Portpatrick & Wigtownshire Joint Committee under LNWR, Midland, Caledonian and G&SW auspices. The last two partners then operated the railway in turn.

The 16 mile Moniaive branch was an altogether more tranquil affair. It opened as a Light Railway on 3rd January 1905 with the intention of serving farming communities near delightful Cairn Water. From Cairn Valley Junction, a couple of miles north of Dumfries, this picturesque line headed for a narrow gap between Killyleoch Hill and Bishop Forest Hill before striking along a more open section of the valley past Dunscore, Wallaceton and Kirkland to the little town of Moniaive.

Early G&SW locomotives, over half of which were built by the company itself, were easily identified at Carlisle because of their domeless boilers. There was a preference for the four-coupled wheel arrangement and an unusually small proportion of tank engines ran on the system. When formed in 1850, the 'Sou'West' had inherited a very motley collection of motive power from the Glasgow, Paisley, Kilmarnock & Ayr Railway, including Kinmond, Hutton & Steel 2-2-2s and Bury 2-2-0s. But the appointment of Patrick Stirling as Locomotive Superintendent in 1853, together with the relocation of the works from Cook Street in Glasgow to larger premises at Kilmarnock, led to a series of 0-4-0s, 0-4-2s and 2-4-0s. Besides domeless boilers, they had round-topped cabs with 'port-hole' side windows and fan-shaped vents in the driving wheel splashers - all hallmarks of the designer.

In 1866 Patrick Stirling went to the Great Northern Railway where he created his legendary 'Singles', his younger brother James taking over at Kilmarnock. New engines of modest proportions perpetuated the characteristics of their predecessors, but a major development was in store. James Stirling introduced his first 4-4-0 in 1873, a wheel arrangement preceded only by Wheatley's pioneers for the North British. From 1876 they performed admirably on Anglo-Scottish expresses, including the heavy 'Pullmans'. Some were still working Ayrshire coast trains well into LMS days.

Stirling resigned in 1878 and was replaced by Hugh Smellie who built a large class of 0-6-0 goods engines, together with more 4-4-0s. He was succeeded by James Manson during 1890. Under the latter's regime a further five classes of 4-4-0s emerged, including a unique four-cylinder loco which was later rebuilt and named LORD GLENARTHUR after the company chairman. Ten handsome 4-6-0s appeared in 1903, followed by another seven in 1910-11. Although they did not entirely eliminate double-heading, these powerful engines included two super-heated examples which regularly exceeded 85mph on the main line. At the other end of the scale, Manson designed some 0-4-4 and 0-6-0 tanks, together with a few short-lived steam rail-motors.

Peter Drummond took up office in 1911 when Manson retired and his output included some large 2-6-0s for the 'Long Road' goods workings from Glasgow to Carlisle via Dalry. Finally, Robert Whitelegge arrived in 1918 and introduced a series of standard boilers for existing locomotives, none too successfully as it turned out. His greatest achievement was a class of six large 4-6-4Ts for heavy Glasgow - Kilmarnock workings. G&SW engines wore a mid-green livery while coaches had a crimson lake finish.

Former G&SW motive power was the first to suffer wholesale slaughter as a result of LMS standardisation. Ex-Midland 2P 4-4-0s and 4F 0-6-0s were brought in and ex-Caledonian types appeared, much to the disgust of older 'Sou' West' men. LMS Compounds and 'Crab' 2-6-0s also became a familiar sight in

With the Southern Uplands looking magnificent in summer sunshine and the well-kept former G&SW station building on the left, Black 5 No.44718 sweeps through Sanquhar with a southbound freight on 27th July 1963. Photograph W.A.C. Smith.

Nithsdale. The last G&SW loco, ironically an 0-6-2T, was withdrawn from Kingmoor in 1948. Jubilees, Rebuilt Scots and Black 5s were common throughout the 1950s and the occasional Pacific was seen towards the end of steam. BR Sulzer 'Peaks' powered most principal trains from the 1960s.

Like the Beattock route, the former G&SW main line survives, but has also been shorn of its branches. Dornock was renamed Eastriggs in May 1923 to avoid confusion with Dornoch on the old Highland system. Remote Rigg station on the Solway plain closed on 1st November 1942 and Moniaive branch passenger services ceased on 3rd May 1943. Cummertrees, another isolated station, finished on 19th September 1955. All trains over the 'Port Road' were withdrawn on 14th June 1965, although Stranraer continued to be served via Ayr and Girvan. Local services between Kilmarnock and Carlisle ended on 6th December 1965, resulting in numerous station closures including Gretna Green, Eastriggs, Ruthwell, Racks and Sanquhar.

Hopefully that was the end of the decline, and Gretna Green and Sanquhar, indeed, have subsequently reopened. Recently, services have been maintained by class 156 Sprinters, providing six or seven trains each weekday between Carlisle and Glasgow. A similar number of short workings venture as far as Dumfries. There is also one train to and from Stranraer via Ayr connecting with Larne and Belfast sailings.

BR Standard 4-6-0 No.73100 restarts the 6.10pm Carlisle - Glasgow St. Enoch from Sanquhar on 27th July 1963. The station closed in 1965 but has since reopened. The local brickworks site has long been cleared. Photograph W.A.C. Smith.

Middle right. On 8th July 1961, Kingmoor 'Clan' Pacific No.72007 CLAN MACKINTOSH makes a punctual 12.02pm pause at Castle Douglas with the 'Stranraer - Larne Boat Train', composed of Gresley stock. Departure from Newcastle had been at 9.00am. Photograph W.A.C. Smith.

Right. Standard class 4MT 2-6-0 No.76072 runs into Castle Douglas with the 12.40 from Kirkcudbright to Dumfries on 19th September 1964. Photograph W.A.C. Smith.

Above. The very impressive North British Atlantics designed by W.P. Reid worked expresses over the Waverley route throughout their existence, until Gresley Pacifics displaced them somewhat prematurely. As LNER class C10, well-polished No.9904 HOLYROOD of St. Margaret's shed shunts a horsebox at Citadel's platform 8 in the late 1920s. Rather oddly, it is carrying an Edinburgh destination board despite facing south. The background is little changed today, but platform 8 is now used mainly for storing stock and No.9904 was scrapped as long ago as 1936. Photograph J.J. Cunningham.

Below. Ex-North British Holmes 4-4-0 No.62059, classified D31 by the LNER, waits at Citadel with a Silloth local in 1949. The veteran became 62281 in 1950 to make way for the numbering sequence allocated to new K1 2-6-0s, but was scrapped in 1952. Note the LNER lettering still adorning the tender. Photograph H.C. Casserley.

Chapter 7
NORTH BRITISH

When the various schemes for a canal across the Pennines from Newcastle foundered, local interests in Carlisle promoted their own 11 mile waterway from a basin on the north west side of the city to a small harbour, at Fisher's Cross alongside the Solway estuary. Work commenced in 1819, the navigation opened in 1823 and the haven was named Port Carlisle. For a couple of decades the Carlisle Canal provided a vital trade link with Ireland and ports along the west coast of England. It even worked in harmony with the Newcastle & Carlisle Railway. Completion of the line to Maryport and Whitehaven and the establishment of a north-south trunk route, however, cast doubts about the future of the local outlet to the sea.

By 1850 the canal was in serious financial difficulty and closure seemed inevitable. This prospect upset some of Carlisle's traders who still wanted a route to the outside world independent of the main line railways. In March 1852, with the backing of the Corporation, they decided to convert the ailing waterway into their own railway. Parliamentary approval for the Port Carlisle Dock & Railway came on 4th August 1853, the channel having been drained three days earlier in anticipation of this decision. Locks were demolished, bridges raised and the basin at Carlisle modified. The result was a most peculiar stretch of track, almost entirely in a cutting and typified by numerous curves and long level stretches punctuated by short sharp gradients where the locks had been. Passenger services to Port Carlisle from the far from romantically-titled Canal station began on 22nd June 1854. Goods traffic in conjunction with the Newcastle & Carlisle branch had commenced a month earlier on 22nd May, with the former canal warehouses adapted for railway purposes.

Sailing vessels entered Port Carlisle harbour with little difficulty, but steamships found the Solway silt a hazard. In consequence, the Port Carlisle company decided to build an extension to Silloth Bay where there was deep water near the shore. The proposal was thrown out of parliament in 1854 as a result of Maryport & Carlisle opposition, but the Carlisle & Silloth Bay Railway & Dock company, with the Mayor of Carlisle as chairman, succeeded in acquiring its Act on 16th July 1855. Construction of the 13 mile route across flat farmland just above sea level was rapid and the line opened on 28th August 1856. Marshall Dock at Silloth was commissioned in August 1859. The backers also envisaged Silloth as a holiday resort, the 'Torquay of the North' according to the Bishop of Carlisle. From 1855 to 1861 some £3,600 of railway money was used to build dwellings, baths, an hotel and other amenities, most of it hidden in the accounts.

Within a couple of years the Port Carlisle and Silloth company finances were in a mess. An indication of this state of affairs was the decision towards the end of 1857 to replace the steam service from Drumburgh to Port Carlisle with a horse-drawn carriage. This may have been a minor local move at the time, but the 'Dandy' subsequently secured an honoured place in British railway history. Meanwhile, trains from the Solway coast continued to terminate at Canal station,

SIR WALTER SCOTT

Citadel could easily be mistaken for somewhere on the LNER main line in this view of the north end, during the 1930s. Gresley A3 Pacific No.2745 CAPTAIN CUTTLE waits on the centre road as a 4-4-0 stands in one of the former North British bays with a local. The Pacific (later BR 60091) was built at Doncaster in 1928 and named after the winner of the 1922 Derby. It went new to Canal shed and remained there for twenty years. Photograph J.F. Ward Collection.

An Illustrated History of Carlisle's Railways

a backwater remote from thriving Citadel. During a series of intrigues and manoeuvres which dominated railway politics in the Borders in the late 1850s and early 1860s, the hapless innocents were rescued from their misery and became the unlikely springing point for a main line to Edinburgh and, eventually, a third Anglo-Scottish trunk route.

The North British Railway began in a modest way during 1846 by running a couple of passenger trains each way between Edinburgh and Berwick over a line which eventually became part of the East Coast route between London and Scotland. Three years later the company completed a branch through the Lothian coalfield to the mill town of Hawick in the Border hills. This was clearly a thinly disguised probe towards Carlisle and it duly rattled the Caledonian board, who promptly started planning their own branch to Hawick from the south, to keep the North British out. Nevertheless, it was the North British which won support in the Border towns, mainly because chairman Richard Hodgson hailed from the area; in fact he became something of a local hero. But years of doubt dogged the project, for south of Hawick lay miles of moorland and thinly populated Liddesdale, neither of which offered much traffic potential. Eventually the Edinburgh directors received a decisive prompt from Derby, 220 miles away. By the late 1850s the Midland Railway had every intention of becoming the third Anglo-Scottish trunk route and needed a partner north of the border to enable it to reach Edinburgh. This dream eventually became reality, but no less than 27 years after the first train drew into Hawick.

The Border Union (North British) Railway Act of 21st July 1859 authorised 43 miles of new track, the bulk of the £5 million venture being the line from Hawick to Carlisle via Riccarton Junction, Newcastleton, Riddings and Longtown. Also sanctioned was a branch from Longtown to Gretna on the Caledonian main line and another from Riddings to Langholm, a town which had welcomed the abortive Caledonian proposal some years earlier. Unfortunately for the North British, the Act stipulated that the main line should not be used for undue competition with the Caledonian for Carlisle - Edinburgh traffic.

Construction through the difficult terrain was made worse by three particularly grim winters, whilst the collapse of a partially completed viaduct added to the problems. There were political drawbacks as well. The North British was fully aware that it would be in enemy territory at Carlisle, for the Caledonian/LNWR West Coast alliance was firmly established by this time. Access to Citadel was assured, but the line from Hawick made a curious approach. It bridged the Caledonian at Kingmoor before joining the

Top. Motive power miscellany at Citadel in September 1961. On the left, A3 Pacific No.60093 CORONACH has arrived at platform 7 with a train from Edinburgh Waverley whilst an unidentified Coronation Pacific is ready to depart from platform 3 with an express for Glasgow Central or Perth. Meanwhile, ex-North British D34 'Glen' 4-4-0 No.62484 GLEN LYON waits impatiently on the centre road. Photograph Neville Stead. *Middle.* A birdseye view of Silloth on 22nd August 1964 with Ivatt mogul No.43040 at the head of the eight-coach 3.05pm departure for Carlisle. The fairly large station building seems lost at the end of the long platform, a reminder of the once lucrative excursion traffic. Lines curve away to the goods yard and docks on the left, whilst Carr's flour mill is in the centre. There was a steamship service from Silloth to Dublin until the outbreak of World War II. Photograph W.A.C. Smith. *Above.* The derelict engine shed at Silloth on 22nd August 1964 as squalls of rain sweep in from the Irish Sea. Ivatt 4MT 2-6-0 No.43040 finishes taking water, prior to working the 3.05pm to Carlisle. Steam had replaced diesel multiple units, but not for long as the traumatic closure day was only a fortnight away. Photograph W.A.C. Smith.

Above. A crew change at Longtown on 6th April 1963. The relief men, having travelled on the 1.40pm Carlisle - Edinburgh hauled by D5311 are about to take over St. Margaret's B1 No.61099 heading a fitted freight from Millerhill to Kingmoor New Yard. The station site, in a village once thronged with munitions workers, has since been cleared. Photograph W.A.C. Smith.

Left. Ivatt class 4MT mogul No.43000 arrives at well-kept Riddings Junction station with the 6.32pm from Langholm to Carlisle on 6th April 1963. The two ex-LMS non-corridor coaches include a rather inappropriate push/pull brake. The remote location of the station is apparent in this view. Photograph W.A.C. Smith.

Bottom. Having left the Waverley route at Riddings Junction, Ivatt class 4MT 2-6-0 No.43000 crosses the border between England and Scotland with the 5.18pm from Carlisle to Langholm on 6th April 1963. Heavy engineering work on the Langholm branch is typified by this viaduct over Liddel Water. Photograph W.A.C. Smith.

still-independent Port Carlisle/Silloth system at Port Carlisle Junction. Just beyond here, use was made of the sharply curving Caledonian goods branch authorised in 1858 and opened in 1860 when that company had plans to take over the minor north Cumberland concerns. For the final mile to Citadel, running powers over the Caledonian main line were granted. This approach may have been unusual, but it soon brought dividends.

Goods traffic between Canal yard and Scotch Dyke at the entrance to Liddesdale began on 15th October 1861 and passenger services from Citadel to Scotch Dyke followed a fortnight later on

Ex-LNER class J39 0-6-0 No.64884 stands at Langholm with a pair of ex-LMS non-corridor coaches forming the 3.28pm to Carlisle on 1st September 1954. The station building with its overhanging eaves was similar to those on the Waverley route, but it has long gone and the site is now marked by a plaque in a housing estate. Photograph W.A.C. Smith.

29th October. The line opened throughout for freight on 23rd June 1862, Edinburgh-Hawick-Carlisle passenger trains commencing soon afterwards on 1st July. It was advertised as the 'Waverley Route' after the novels of Sir Walter Scott - which were largely based in the territory through which the line passed - and the name remained popular for over a century.

Goods traffic over the branch from Longtown to Gretna began on 15th October 1861 and passenger workings started at the same time as the through service from Edinburgh to Carlisle. Although the North British had its own platform at Gretna, trains tended to continue to Gretna Green on the Glasgow & South Western via the Caledonian station, thus using the facilities of three different companies in a very short distance. The Langholm branch opened for traffic on 18th April 1864.

The West Coast partners had a secret agreement to send all Edinburgh goods traffic via Carstairs, unless the Waverley route was clearly specified. This meant that even some wagons carrying materials for internal North British use were travelling north over the Caledonian! Fortunately the company was able to fight back effectively. It had leased the Port Carlisle and Silloth Bay lines on 3rd June 1862 and soon developed a link from Edinburgh to Liverpool using its own steamers out of Silloth. This completely avoided foreign mileage and won a lot of business by undercutting the competition.

It was not so easy on the passenger side, and Edinburgh trains were regularly delayed at Carlisle until the Caledonian service had departed. Hefty tolls were demanded for access to Citadel and running powers north of the station, resulting in prolonged litigation and eventual arbitration. All this helped to make the Waverley route uneconomic and there were bitter arguments in the North British boardroom. Certain directors even wanted the line sold off to any company willing to purchase it. Salvation came with the opening of the Settle & Carlisle in 1876. Although Edinburgh - St Pancras expresses had no great impact on East Coast traffic, they provided a direct service from the Border towns to London and were popular for journeys from the Scottish capital to the West Riding and East Midlands. The trains also boasted luxurious rolling stock and this tempted Edinburgh - London passengers who were in no great hurry.

After leaving the Caledonian route at Port Carlisle Branch Junction and negotiating Canal Junction, Edinburgh trains curved north across the River Eden then headed north eastwards, spanning the main line near Kingmoor House. Low lying open farmland followed, with stations provided at Harker (4$\frac{1}{2}$ miles out of Citadel) and Lyneside (6$\frac{3}{4}$ miles). Bridges over the Rivers Lyne and Esk led to Longtown (9$\frac{3}{4}$ miles). At this point the rails were still less than 50ft above sea level, but the relentless climb into the Southern Uplands soon commenced.

Scotch Dyke station, 12 miles from Citadel and about 100ft up, stood in a remote spot near extensive parkland forming the Netherby estate. The Waverley route entered Liddesdale at Riddings (14 miles) and kept to the south of Liddel Water, thus remaining in England. A steady ascent encountered an increasingly lonely but beautiful landscape. Penton (16$\frac{3}{4}$ miles and altitude 250ft) was above the river in its wooded gorge. At Kershope Foot (21$\frac{1}{4}$ miles) the line finally entered Scotland and soon crossed to the west side of Liddel Water.

By Newcastleton, an almost unexpected grey stone town amid bleak hills, trains had travelled 24$\frac{1}{4}$ miles from Carlisle and were 350 ft above the Solway. The climb then began in earnest. Isolated Steele Road station (28$\frac{3}{4}$ miles) was 600ft up and wild moors stretched away to 1,862ft Roan Fell to the west and 1,679ft Larriston Fell to the east. Ahead lay Riccarton Junction (32$\frac{1}{4}$ miles), Whitrope summit (970 ft) and the descent through the Border textile towns.

North British branches in the Carlisle area encountered varied topography. That from Longtown to Gretna ambled across the flat Esk flood plain for three miles. The seven-mile Riddings - Langholm line twisted along the side of the deep Esk valley and required viaducts over Liddel Water, Byre Burn and Tarras Water. Silloth trains first encountered severe curves at Knockupworth and Kirkandrews inherited from the Carlisle Canal, then followed the old sea wall to Drumburgh and finally struck across reclaimed marshland for thirteen miles, barely reaching 50ft at its highest point.

The Cumbrian coast branches experienced many changes. Firstly, a station called Port Carlisle Junction opened at the convergence of the Waverley route in July 1863 for interchange purposes. It closed on 1st July 1864 when Silloth passenger services were diverted to Citadel and Canal became goods only. Silloth docks prospered as coal exports boomed, imports of Irish cattle and horses increased, and copious amounts of flour for Carlisle's biscuit industry were unloaded. However, the North British began to lose interest in its English port when the Settle & Carlisle opened and a friendly outlet to the south was assured. The Port Carlisle and Silloth lines were finally absorbed by the Scottish company on 12th August 1880.

An upturn in fortunes came during 1885 when the six-acre New Dock opened at Silloth and Carr's colossal flour mill was built. (The firm's Carlisle biscuit factory had been established alongside the canal as long ago as 1831.) During Edwardian times Silloth enjoyed a revival as a resort and became a favourite escape for the residents of Carlisle. World War 1 saw the establishment of a gun-testing range near the terminus and this provided further traffic.

Back at Carlisle, it was the usual practice to divide Anglo-Scottish trains from Leeds and the south into Glasgow and Edinburgh portions at first. But the upsurge in traffic after the Forth Bridge opened meant that they tended to run as separate trains from 1890. When Settle & Carlisle services began, the North British could not come up with sufficiently powerful engines for working expresses forward over the Waverley route. This situation was rectified a couple of years later when Dugald Drummond's 4-4-0s emerged from Cowlairs works in Glasgow. They were the largest and most powerful four-coupled locos in Britain at the time and dominated the Carlisle - Edinburgh line for two decades. By covering the 98 miles in 2 hours 10 minutes with heavy Pullman trains they also became world famous.

Matthew Holmes introduced a further batch of 4-4-0s in 1898 and W P Reid's Atlantic 4-4-2s appeared on the Waverley route in 1906, with No 876 WAVERLEY soon a regular sight at Citadel. The Scott 4-4-0s appeared in 1909, followed by the Glen 4-4-0s during 1913. North British passenger engines were painted a very dark yellow, while coaches carried a deep purple-red livery. Meanwhile, pensioned-off 4-4-0s worked the Silloth and Langholm branches. The final run of England's last horse-drawn passenger service - from Port Carlisle to Drumburgh - was in April 1914 when steam traction took over again. After sinking into a derelict state following sundry non-railway use, the 'Dandy' was rescued and restored. It is now a treasured exhibit at York Museum.

In LNER days, Nigel Gresley tended to keep the newer pre-grouping engines he inherited rather than replace them with standard types, as was LMS policy, so the Scotts and Glens continued to run into Carlisle throughout the 1920s and 1930s. However, new A3 Pacifics were introduced on Waverley route expresses and these proved most successful. Under British Railways auspices the A3s, together with V2 2-6-2s, virtually monopolised the Edinburgh - Carlisle route until ousted by BR/Sulzer Type 4 'Peak' diesels in 1961. Birmingham RCW Type 2s worked stopping services. Even so, ex-LNER J39 0-6-0s hauled most Silloth and Langholm branch trains until 1962.

Virtually all former North British tracks around Carlisle have disappeared, unlike those of the other six pre-grouping companies. The process began on 9th August 1915 when the somewhat unnecessary Longtown - Gretna passenger service was withdrawn. Ironically, part of the branch has outlived the rest of the local North British system as it serves the adjacent munitions depot. From 1st January 1917 to 1st February 1919 the Port Carlisle line was closed completely, as a wartime economy measure. Remote Harker and Lyneside stations lost their passenger services on 1st November 1929. In the same year a Sentinel steam railcar began to work the Port Carlisle branch, but the line was a lost cause and all facilities were withdrawn on 1st June 1932.

Scotch Dyke station closed on 2nd May 1949 and Drumburgh, erstwhile junction for Port Carlisle, expired on 4th July 1955. Mayhem, literally, followed in the wake of the Beeching report. An early casualty was the Langholm branch passenger service, terminated with little protest on 15th June 1964. Silloth was a very

Top. **B1 4-6-0 No.61242 sweeps down Liddesdale towards Riddings Junction with a southbound Waverley route freight on 6th April 1963. The attractive but hardly lucrative nature of much of the line is apparent in this view. Photograph W.A.C. Smith.**

Above. **Class V2 2-6-2 No.60840 breasts Whitrope summit as it heads south with an express freight over the Waverley route on 8th July 1961. In the background, bleak moorland with the rather homely name Sandy Edge marks the watershed between Liddesdale and Teviotdale as well as the point where the Cheviot Hills merge with the Southern Uplands. Whitrope tunnel was bored through the ridge. Photograph G.W. Morrison.**

different matter. All seemed well in 1962 when Irish cattle were still being transferred from ships to railway wagons in the docks and the introduction of diesel multiple units apparently heralded a bright future. Suddenly, the withdrawal of passenger trains was announced for 7th September 1964. On the last evening a jeering crowd estimated at several thousand gathered at the terminus. There was a mass sit-down on the tracks and stones were thrown at a railway inspector.

At the time the Waverley route was also under threat. A decade earlier again all had seemed well, with the St Pancras - Edinburgh through train being christened 'The Waverley' and A3s based at Canal shed taking over from Leeds engines in time-honoured fashion. But on 6th January 1969 the line from Carlisle to the Scottish capital also closed, together with 21 Borders and Lothian stations. The last train, an up sleeper, suffered considerable delay at Newcastleton in scenes reminiscent of those at Silloth a few years earlier. Although Carlisle was not affected by the demise of the Waverley route, it was a real setback to towns such as Hawick, Melrose and Galashiels. Fortunately, it is possible to end on a slightly brighter note, as currently plans are well advanced for relaying a line from Kingmoor to Riccarton, for transporting timber from Kielder Forest.

Above. Quintessential Midland double-heading around 1920. Class 2 4-4-0 No.431 and class 4 Compound 4-4-0 No.1009 depart from Carlisle with an up express. North British Atlantic No.905 BUCCLEUCH, which may well have hauled the train from Edinburgh, looks on. Photograph J. F. Ward Collection.

Below. The Jubilees brought a much-needed boost to Settle & Carlisle motive power. No.45613 KENYA backs out from platform 4 at Citadel on 18th September 1956. An interesting feature is the early Stanier high-sided tender, only ten of which were built. Photograph F.W. Shuttleworth.

Chapter 8
MIDLAND

The last main line to reach Carlisle has become one of the great legends of British railway history. Indeed, many people with little or no knowledge of trains have at least heard of the Settle & Carlisle. An enormous amount has been written about the Midland's route across the high Pennines; nevertheless a brief portrait of this superb piece of Victorian engineering is essential here. The 72 mile line featured no less than twenty viaducts and fourteen tunnels as well as numerous massive earthworks. It was surveyed by men of vision who managed to find a way, suitable for expresses, along lonely valleys and across high, bleak moors. Then it was turned into reality by workers using time-honoured methods dating back to the canal era.

George Hudson has already been mentioned in connection with the Newcastle & Carlisle and Maryport & Carlisle. In 1844 he instigated the first large scale railway amalgamation in the country when three independent concerns based on Derby were welded together to form the Midland Railway. The new company had lines radiating to Leeds, Rugby and Hampton in Arden, but was far from content being confined to the centre of England. With a burning ambition backed by highly competent management and a healthy bank balance brought about by lucrative coal traffic, the Midland eventually reached London, Manchester, Liverpool, Bristol, South Wales, Bournemouth, Yarmouth and, of course, Carlisle.

As early as 1852-53 there was talk of amalgamation, first with the LNWR, then with both the LNWR and Great Northern. However, Parliament was alarmed by the prospect of such huge conglomerates and the plans were quashed. So the Midland embarked on its relentless expansion programme. Tired of handing over its London traffic to the LNWR at Rugby, the company built a line from Leicester to Hitchin on the Great Northern, the first Midland expresses from Kings Cross to the north running in 1858. By then, the idea of becoming a third Anglo-Scottish trunk route had firmly taken root.

PENYGHENT

The quest for Scotland was made slightly easier by a ready-made springing point, in the shape of the Leeds & Bradford Railway. This opened in 1846 and thrust out a branch to Skipton the following year. It was bought by the Midland in 1851. Then came the saga of the North Western Railway, which was unofficially given the prefix 'Little' to distinguish it from the much larger West Coast company. The original plan was to build a main line from Skipton to Low Gill on the Lancaster & Carlisle and a branch from Clapham to Lancaster. However,

On 10th September 1960 there was a reminder of the Midland's double-heading practice, albeit with considerably more drawbar pull on offer. Class 5 4-6-0 No.45481 and Royal Scot 4-6-0 No.46117 WELSH GUARDSMAN leave Citadel with the southbound 'Waverley' express (10.05am Edinburgh - St. Pancras). One of the pilot's 841 classmates, No.45452, stands on the extreme left. Photograph W.A.C. Smith.

Top. Running 22 minutes late because of a diesel failure south of Leeds, the 09.20 from St. Pancras to Glasgow arrives at Carlisle on 22nd July 1967 with Britannia Pacific No.70016 ARIEL in charge. Although diagrammed for steam haulage, the train was taken forward by a Type 4 diesel. Photograph W.A.C. Smith.

Above. The up 'Waverley' at Carlisle around 1960 with Bank Hall unrebuilt 'Patriot' No.45517 in charge. In the background, immediately to the right of the engine, is the preserved horse-drawn 'Dandy' car from the Port Carlisle branch. Photograph Neville Stead Collection.

when the Little North Western materialised in 1849-50 it comprised a through route from Skipton to Lancaster, with a branch from Clapham to Ingleton, well short of Low Gill.

This minor north Yorkshire company immediately became embroiled in the cold war between the Midland and LNWR. To complicate matters, it was also wooed by the Great Northern, which wanted an independent route to Scotland too. So the Midland offered to work the Little North Western in 1852 and leased the railway during 1859. At the same time the Lancaster & Carlisle found itself being coveted by Derby, but could not face the inevitable Parliamentary wrangling and pledged itself to Euston. In 1861 the LNWR opened a line from Low Gill to Ingleton along the Little North Western alignment proposed earlier. After several months of mutual antipathy at Ingleton, tempers cooled and through Midland coaches between King's Cross and Glasgow passed this way.

Despite these arrangements, the Midland announced its intention to build a rival route to Scotland. The LNWR was perturbed and entered into discussions about joint ownership of the Lancaster - Carlisle section, but these rambled on and finally broke down in 1865. A Bill for the Settle & Carlisle was therefore presented to Parliament the following year. With very strong, almost passionate backing from the North British, Lancashire & Yorkshire and G&SW, the Midland acquired its Act for the new railway on 16th July 1866. During the following session there was an attempt to amalgamate with the G&SW, but this was rejected by the Commons.

Meanwhile there was growing disquiet among shareholders about the scale of the venture and they persuaded the Midland board to reconsider it. After all, a lot of money was already being spent on the Bedford - St Pancras extension. Negotiations were resumed with the LNWR and in 1868 an agreement was reached about access to the West Coast main line north of Lancaster. So another Bill was presented to Parliament, with the aim of terminating the Settle & Carlisle project. This time the passion of the Lancashire & Yorkshire and North British was directed against the Midland and the abandonment attempt was thrown out. Derby was thus required to build a railway across the Pennines it neither wanted nor needed.

Fortunately, the company took its obligations seriously and with a corporate shrug of the shoulders proceeded to build a main line from Settle Junction, on the former Little North Western, to Petteril Bridge Junction, on the erstwhile Newcastle & Carlisle, to the highest possible standards. J S Crossley, the Midland's engineer since 1857, was due to retire but stayed on to oversee the huge task. By 1871 no less than 7,000 navvies were at work on the alignment and they often had to contend with the most difficult conditions imaginable. On the higher sections, tough limestone and deep bogs caused endless problems; lower down there were piles of glacial deposits which became a slithering slurry when wet. Cloying mist, driving rain, relentless blizzards and cutting winds were all too common and caused many men to abandon the shanty towns on the moors to seek an easier way of earning a living.

The line should have been completed in 1873, but the first goods train to cover the whole route did not actually run until 2nd August 1875. Passenger services commenced on 1st May 1876 and an excited throng gathered at Citadel to watch the first Midland express arrive. No doubt this caused all manner of interest, consisting as it did of several large and stately American Pullman coaches with relatively small 2-4-0s in charge. There was no official ceremony. Maybe the board felt that it had already spent enough on the Settle & Carlisle - the original estimate was less than £2½ million, but the final bill was not far off £4 million!

Regular services in the early years included half a dozen expresses from St Pancras to Carlisle, two of which were through trains to both Glasgow and Edinburgh, via the G&SW and North British routes respectively. The Settle & Carlisle was built primarily for such work-

An Illustrated History of Carlisle's Railways

Top. Peak No.D29 hauling the up 'Waverley' threads the complex of lines south of Citadel on 6th April 1963 as a Black 5 heads towards the station with a train of vans. In the foreground, from left to right, are the goods tracks from Upperby Junction and London Road Junction to Bog Junction, then the passenger lines from Petteril Bridge Junction (being used by the Peak). The bridge nearest the camera carried the branch to Crown Street goods, then there is the West Coast main line (being used by the Black 5) and beyond it, out of sight, the Maryport & Carlisle bridge. Photograph W.A.C. Smith.

Above. Britannia Pacific No.70009 ALFRED THE GREAT approaches London Road Junction with the 4.37pm local from Carlisle to Bradford Forster Square on 8th May 1965. The spur to Upperby goes off to the left. Photograph W.A.C. Smith.

ings and there was only ever a handful of stopping passenger trains. With eleven more route miles to cover and the Pennines to climb, the Midland journey from London was an hour longer than that over the LNWR. For many travellers this was far more than offset by the scenic splendour outside the carriage and the unabashed luxury within; the Pullmans were just the first of a series of magnificent coaches.

No doubt hankering after the 1850s and 1860s when they had a stranglehold on passenger traffic through Carlisle, the LNWR and Caledonian set out to obstruct Midland business in the city, mirroring the contempt shown earlier for the G&SW and North British. By 1882 Derby was losing patience and promoted its own Bill with a view to becoming a member of the Joint Committee. Malpractice concerning traffic control came under the spotlight and the West Coast alliance had to mend their ways. At long last there was a spirit of co-operation at Citadel - no mean feat for a station used by seven companies. This enabled the Midland, G&SW and North British to take full advantage of the bounteous late Victorian and Edwardian years.

Although they were bound for the most spectacular railway route in England, Midland expresses did not stand out as anything special at Carlisle. True, there was the beautiful red livery and sumptuous rolling stock, but the size of the station, together with an endless procession of trains in a rich variety of colours, lessened the impact. Furthermore, the way out of the Border City consisted of an amble along North Eastern tracks, as far as Petteril Bridge Junction.

The assault on the Pennines began in a very modest way, with a curve to the south through Scotby (2½ miles from Citadel and just 150ft above sea level), followed by a gentle ascent through Cumwhinton (3¾ miles). The curiously named Pow Maughan stream accompanied the line to Cotehill (6½ miles), then the tracks made their way along the Eden gorge for nearly eight miles. High Stand Gill viaduct and Drybeck viaduct spanned minor streams which had cut clefts into the side of the valley. Armathwaite, a little village which boasted a castle, was provided with a station 10 miles out of Citadel. By now the line had climbed to 300ft above sea level and was still more or less at this altitude eight miles later, despite a series of modest switchbacks. Engineering work increased markedly, with Armathwaite viaduct, Armathwaite tunnel and Baron Wood tunnels following in quick succession. This was an extremely attractive section of the route, affording delightful views of steep wooded slopes tumbling down to the Eden.

Next came Lazonby & Kirkoswald station (15¼ miles); the latter village also possessed a small castle. Lazonby tunnel was followed by Eden Lacy viaduct which carried the railway to the east bank of the river. The structure was sometimes called Long Meg viaduct after Long Meg and Her Daughters, a nearby prehistoric stone circle said to equal Stonehenge in importance. The anhydrite mine and works next to the line was a principal source of freight traffic for decades. More open country typified the upper part of the Eden valley as Settle & Carlisle trains encountered Little Salkeld station (18¼ miles), Dodd's Mill viaduct, Langwathby station (19¾ miles), Waste Bank tunnel, Culgaith tunnel, Culgaith station (23¼ miles) and Crowdundle viaduct, where the 400ft contour was crossed.

Five miles away to the north east, the high Pennines were evident in the form of Melmerby Fell, with its white limestone scars and bulky Cross Fell, rising to 2,930 ft. Newbiggin (24¾ miles) and Long Marton (27¾ miles) were passed before the train rolled into Appleby. The station at this old market town was 520ft above sea level and nearly thirty one miles from Citadel, yet the LNWR main line was only eight miles away to the west. However, the Lancaster & Carlisle route had almost reached Shap summit and the Midland still had a great deal of climbing to do. The ascent began in earnest alongside the Helm Beck, then through increasingly remote sheep pastures dotted with isolated farms and stone barns. Ahead lay Kirkby Stephen (860ft up and 41½ miles

51

from Citadel) and the 1,169ft summit at Ais Gill just under 48 miles from the Border City. There were also those wild and fascinating places with names which became synonymous with the Settle & Carlisle: Mallerstang, Garsdale, Dent Head, Blea Moor, Whernside, Ribblehead, Ingleborough and Pen-y-Ghent.

As far as the overall concept was concerned, Midland architecture north of Settle had little in common with local vernacular tradition. Buildings showed a remarkable degree of uniformity and reflected a style which gradually evolved while J S Crossley was in office. Even company houses at the remotest locations had more than a hint of Derby gothic about them. However, the stations were neither over elaborate nor unduly plain and somehow seemed to celebrate a major engineering triumph while reflecting the wild nature of the terrain. Indeed, they became a familiar and almost quintessential aspect of this line through the Pennines.

Apart from Hawes Junction and Culgaith, all passenger buildings featured projecting gabled pavilions at right angles to the platforms with wings and linking sections parallel to the track. All structures were single-storey and came in three sizes according to the status of the particular settlement served. Fretted bargeboards were employed and there was frequent use of decorative iron and glass screens incorporating diamond-shaped panes along the platform elevation of the waiting room. Some homage was paid to the changing nature of the route by the use of local construction materials - red sandstone at Armathwaite and gritstone at Dent, for example. Scotby had the distinction of being the most northerly station on the Midland system (the most southerly in which the company had an interest being Bailey Gate on the Somerset & Dorset Joint, just north of Poole in Dorset!)

In Midland days the Settle & Carlisle saw a succession of elegant yet relatively small express passenger locomotives, and every new design - with the exception of the famous 4-2-2 'Spinners' - served in the Pennines. When the line opened, Samuel Waite Johnson had just taken over from Matthew Kirtley as Locomotive Superintendent and the latter's outside-framed 2-4-0s were soon joined by similar engines from his successor. Then came a couple of batches of 4-4-0s which were not much larger than the 2-4-0s. Johnson eventually designed a more powerful 4-4-0 with the Carlisle road in mind. The first five went to Leeds Holbeck shed in 1900 specifically for these duties, but before long no less than eighty of them could be found all over the Midland network. During 1902 the first of the highly successful Compound 4-4-0s appeared. When Richard Deeley was appointed the following year he decided to build a further 29 Compounds, together with ten conventional 4-4-0s (the '999' class) which spent virtually all their time on the Settle & Carlisle. Afterwards Deeley concentrated on rebuilding Johnson's engines so that they could cope with increasingly heavy trains. Meanwhile, Thomas Clayton and David Bain had been designing the finest carriages in the country for the Midland's Anglo-Scottish services. The beautiful crimson lake livery for locomotives and coaches alike became legendary. On the goods side matters were rather simpler, virtually all traffic being handled by a series of Kirtley, Johnson, Deeley and Fowler 0-6-0s.

When the LMS inherited the Midland in 1923, all Carlisle expresses were hauled by 4-4-0s, more often than not piloted by another 4-4-0 or even a 2-4-0. The new company continued the Midland tradition by building another 195 Compounds in the 1920s - these proved the death knell for many ex-G&SW engines as noted earlier. Furthermore, the distinctive red livery was perpetuated in modified form and was even applied over that ethereal Caledonian blue paintwork. However, the Grouping meant that the rival routes over Shap and Ais Gill were placed under common management. Inevitably, this heralded a gradual decline for the latter as a main passenger line. There seemed little hope of developing local traffic either; after all, the only intermediate places of any significance - Appleby and Kirkby Stephen - were even served by other railways.

At first the LMS used the Settle & Carlisle as a test bed for 'foreign' engines including ex-LNWR 4-6-0s and ex-Caledonian 4-4-0s, but most traffic remained in the hands of Compounds and superheated ex-Midland 4-4-0s. New Royal Scots went to the West Coast main line, the route to Leeds having to make do with a few displaced Claughtons. There was a real improvement at last when Jubilee 4-6-0s were introduced in 1936. In fact these engines remained characteristic of the line until the end of steam some thirty years later. Another infusion of top link power came in 1943 when several rebuilt Royal Scots began working from Leeds to Carlisle. Freight traffic north of Settle actually increased in LMS days. The venerable 0-6-0s were gradually replaced by larger 4Fs of the same wheel arrangement; 'Crab' 2-6-0s arrived soon after Grouping, to be followed by Stanier 8F 2-8-0s.

There was some reason for optimism shortly after Nationalisation when the principal Glasgow - St Pancras train was named the 'Thames-Clyde Express' in 1950. The Edinburgh equivalent subsequently became known as the 'Waverley'. In 1951 Standard Britannia Pacific No.70016 ARIEL was tried over the Settle & Carlisle but proved ineffective. Instead, the diet of Jubilees, rebuilt Scots and Black 5s continued and even 2P 4-4-0s were used as pilots until 1961. The 1960s proved a decade of change, with displaced Gresley A3 Pacifics, Standard 9F 2-10-0s and BR/Sulzer 'Peak' diesels mingling with traditional ex-LMS motive power. When Leeds Holbeck Jubilees No 45562 ALBERTA and No 45593 KOLHAPUR had their swansong on the 06.40 from Birmingham and down relief 'Thames-Clyde Express' on summer Saturdays during 1967, they attracted a fanatical following.

A cloud other than those often shrouding Ingleborough and Pen-y-Ghent hung over the former Midland main line from the early 1960s, despite the decision

'Jubilee' 4-6-0 No.45593 KOLHAPUR passes the back yards of London Road as it rolls into Carlisle with the 09.20 from St. Pancras to Glasgow on 12th August 1967. The spur from London Road Junction to Upperby goes off to the right. Photograph W.A.C. Smith.

52

Above. Class 5 4-6-0 No.44910 passes Durranhill with the lightweight 13.10 freight to Skipton on 28th October 1967, two months before the end of steam working from Carlisle. Photograph W.A.C. Smith.

Below. Drystone walls, coarse grass and a backdrop of bleak but magnificent hills typified the higher reaches of the Settle & Carlisle. With Wild Boar Fell towering above the train, Jubilee No.45562 ALBERTA lifts the up 'Waverley' express towards Ais Gill summit on 13th July 1961. Photograph G.W. Morrison.

to divert most West Coast freight traffic this way in 1970. The three stations nearest Carlisle had already closed - Scotby on 1st February 1942, Cotehill on 7th April 1952 and Cumwhinton on 5th November 1956. A plan to withdraw all stopping trains was thrown out by the Minister of Transport in 1964, but all intermediate stations with the exception of Appleby and Settle succumbed on 4th May 1970. The railway then experienced nearly two decades of uncertainty. Five local stations in the hills reopened during the summer of 1975 for 'Dalesrail' charter excursions but by this time the 'Thames-Clyde' had followed the 'Waverley' into history. In May 1982 the through Glasgow - Nottingham train finished and it looked like the end was imminent. A closure notice was issued on 17th November 1983, but this precipitated a ferocious national campaign to save the line, the like of which had never been seen before. The complete withdrawal of services was advertised for 16th October 1989, but the Secretary of State for Transport intervened and more or less ordered British Rail to develop the railway. With six trains each way calling at ten intermediate stations in 1997, the massive protest was clearly worthwhile.

Carlisle Citadel Station

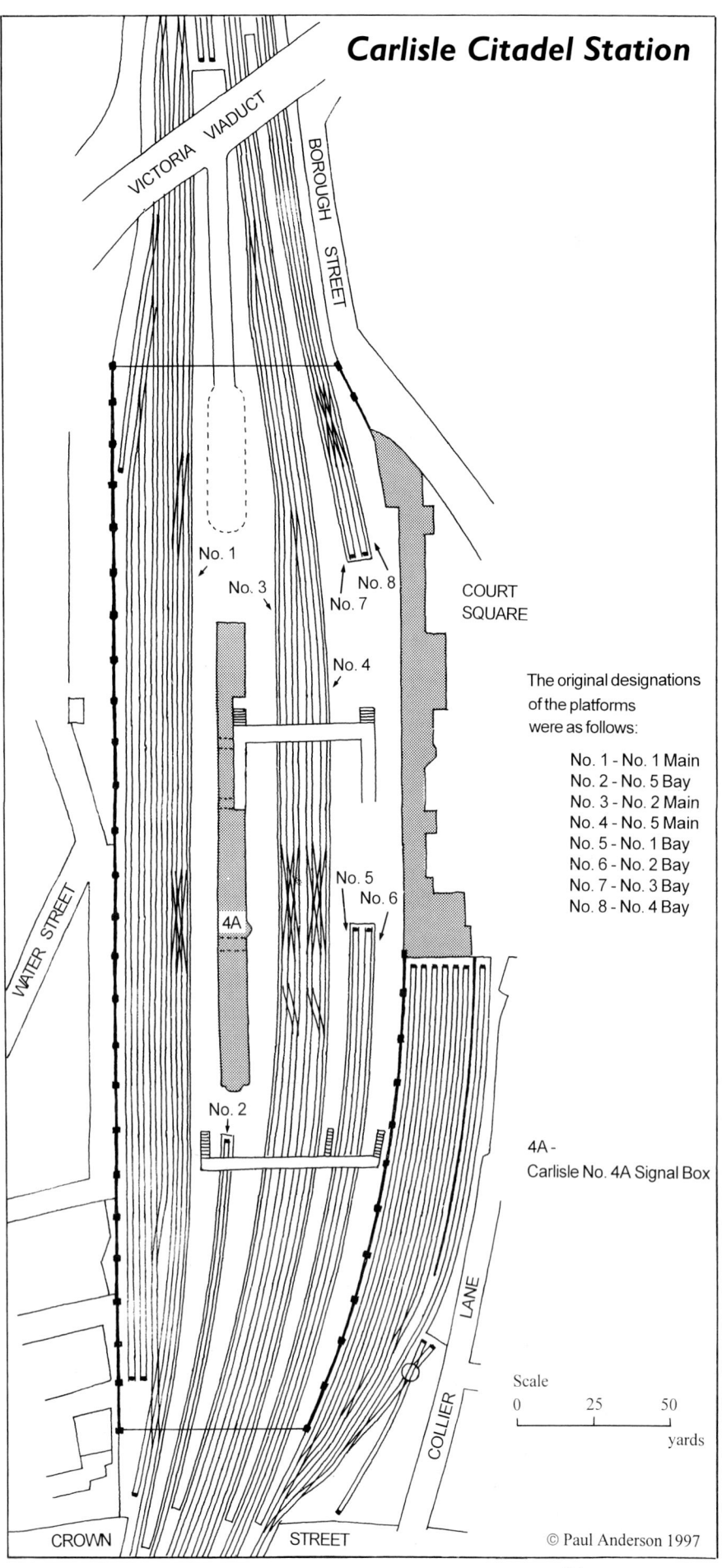

The original designations of the platforms were as follows:

No. 1 - No. 1 Main
No. 2 - No. 5 Bay
No. 3 - No. 2 Main
No. 4 - No. 5 Main
No. 5 - No. 1 Bay
No. 6 - No. 2 Bay
No. 7 - No. 3 Bay
No. 8 - No. 4 Bay

4A - Carlisle No. 4A Signal Box

© Paul Anderson 1997

Carlisle Citadel was unique - certainly in Britain and probably throughout the world. There have been larger stations, more efficient stations, busier stations and more architecturally revered stations. Furthermore, Citadel ranks fairly low in the general public perception of 'great' railway establishments - it does not spring to the tongue like a Waterloo or a Kings Cross. What made the place so special was that it accommodated seven different railway companies under one roof and several of them were bitter rivals. Initially, there was much antagonism, as noted earlier, but from the early 1880s a certain degree of harmonious co-habitation prevailed. The variety of locomotives, rolling stock, liveries and train services made it a Mecca for enthusiasts and some of the magic was still there as late as the 1960s.

As described in Chapter 2, there were passenger facilities in Carlisle well before the opening of Citadel - the Newcastle & Carlisle station at London Road, somewhat grand for its day, opened in

Chapter 9
CITADEL

1836. Seven years later, the Maryport & Carlisle submitted plans for a substantial terminus at Crown Street, but these were rejected by Parliament during the 1843 session. In 1844 the situation changed completely when the Lancaster & Carlisle was authorised and plans for the Caledonian were well advanced. There was already talk of a single station to serve the Border City, although inevitably this would be arranged to cater for north - south traffic, which looked set to eclipse the existing east - west flows.

The Lancaster & Carlisle entered into discussions with the Caledonian, Newcastle & Carlisle and Maryport & Carlisle to determine the best site. Court Square, adjacent to the Citadel, emerged as the favoured location and initially both the Caledonian and Newcastle & Carlisle seemed happy with the choice. However,

THE CITADEL IN VICTORIAN TIMES

Sir William Tite's superb Tudor gothic entrance building at Carlisle Citadel, seen in 1953. The arcade, with spaces for coats of arms above the five arches, can be seen to the left of the tower. Although the 1881 train shed is considerably higher than the original structure, it blends well with the late 1840s architecture.

An Illustrated History of Carlisle's Railways

The interior of Citadel, looking north from the footbridge in 1953, with an ex-LMS Compound biding its time at platform 3. A B1 has arrived in bay No.8 with a local train, although it is barely visible behind the empty stock in No.7. The transverse roof, northern end screen and supporting walls virtually envelop the platforms.

the Maryport company wanted to be in control of its own affairs and succeeded in gaining permission for its Crown Street station at the same time as the Lancaster & Carlisle was approved. But the approach line was not sanctioned and this resulted in the demolition saga some years later (Chapter 3). Before long, the Newcastle & Carlisle began to have doubts as well.

When the Caledonian obtained its Act in 1845 the need to finalise arrangements for a common station became paramount, so the Court Square site was purchased and a Joint Committee formed.

The interior of Citadel, looking south in 1953. A Compound is about to remove a rake of Gresley coaches from platform 4, a Settle & Carlisle local brought in by a Jubilee is unloading at bay No.5, and a B1 backs out of platform 6 after its Newcastle coaches had been drawn clear. The scissors crossings are very clear in this view.

Puddles of rainwater on platform 3 reveal the run down condition of the roof in this study of Citadel, at 10.40am on 5th May 1955. At the south end an A3 Pacific stands on one of the centre roads, a B1 waits at platform 5 with a Newcastle train and a 4F 0-6-0 is about to amble through with a short freight.

Contributions towards the cost of the project were requested from the established companies, but none materialised and negotiations broke down. Acrimoniously, the Lancaster & Carlisle and Caledonian informed the Maryport & Carlisle and Newcastle & Carlisle that if they ever wished to use the new facilities it would be as tenants rather than joint proprietors. The former was quite content to stay at Crown Street, while the former decided to remain at London Road.

An unusual prospect of Citadel at 8.30am on 9th June 1953, looking across to the island platform from up main No.4. Note the elegant Tudor window of signal cabin 4A above the centre suburban coach, M16488.

Sunlight, steam and shadows at the south end of Citadel on 9th June 1953. A 3F 0-6-0T shunts empty stock as part of its station pilot duties and a named B1 waits alongside platform 4.

The budding West Coast partners therefore pressed ahead on their own and obtained an Act for the Court Square station, on 27th July 1846. 'Citadel' was an appropriate and distinctive suffix for the new venture and seems to have been applied from the outset. There was a flurry of potential competition when George Hudson responded by proposing a joint Maryport & Carlisle/Newcastle & Carlisle station just south of Crown Street. This would also welcome the North British and what became the Glasgow & South Western, should they ever reach Carlisle. Hudson's decline, together with a lack of fi-

Class 5MT 4-6-0 No.45299 backs out of platform 3 on 9th June 1953, its driver casting a dour glance at the photographer. The Maryport & Carlisle bay is in the foreground and the steam on the left is from the 0-6-0T station pilot.

Royal Scot 4-6-0 No.46120 ROYAL INNISKILLING FUSILIER blows of steam at the north end of platform 1 and a J39 0-6-0 lurks in the distance beyond platform 3, on 9th June 1953. Note how the end screen accommodates the ramp up to Victoria Viaduct. Two of the colour lights installed during the signalling work of 1951 can be seen on the right.

nance, ensured that the idea was a non starter.

Work began on Citadel towards the end of 1846. Ramshackle houses and workshops were cleared and the station began to take shape over the ensuing nine months, although it was far from complete when the first passenger trains arrived early in September 1847. The opening date has been quoted as 1st September, but there is no conclusive documentary evidence that Lancaster & Carlisle services were diverted from London Road on this particular day. Caledonian trains certainly used the station when the line from Beattock opened on 10th September. The precise events of the previous week or so seem lost in the mists of time.

Two ex-LNWR 0-6-0s, Nos.8318 and 8428, wait for the road at the south end of Carlisle station. The intricate nature of the end screen is clearly visible in this 7th August 1938 view. Photograph L. Hanson.

59

The north end of Citadel, around 1955, with Kingmoor 4F 0-6-0 No.43922 on pilot duty and an A3 Pacific waiting to depart from platform 1 with an Edinburgh Waverley train. Nowhere else did carriage sidings have such a magnificent roof. The combination of gothic and Tudor styles for the timberwork gave the end screen its character. However, missing and broken windows, together with a mantle of grime, signalled the end for this gem of Victorian architecture. Photograph Neville Stead Collection.

Designed throughout by Sir William Tite, Citadel was finally completed in 1850. It consisted of two side platforms served by two through lines with three sidings between them. Access to the down platform was by means of a subway. The train shed, 560ft long by 120ft wide, consisted of three longitudinal iron and glass gables, supported in the middle by two rows of iron columns between the tracks. At its western extremity the overall roof sprang from a screen wall at the back of the outer platform, but on the Court Square side it was attached to the main building - a wonderful edifice which is still the pride of the station a century and a half later.

Sir William Tite was one of the few really important Victorian architects to undertake more than the occasional showpiece for a railway company, as noted in Chapter 4. After creating the astonishingly flamboyant terminus at Gosport in 1841, he went on to design humble Tudor cottages for the Lancaster & Carlisle. At Carlisle itself he used Victorian Tudor to magnificent effect in what was by far the finest station of the time in north west England.

Citadel was provided with an irregular two-storey frontage of considerable length, its centrepiece a clock tower capped by an octagonal lantern. To the left of it was a five-bay entrance arcade with heavy buttresses. Similar features extended upwards between mullioned first floor windows, culminating in slender, crenallated shafts. Space was reserved above each of the entrance arches for an heraldic device. The centre spot boasted the royal coat of arms and this was flanked by the arms of the Lancaster & Carlisle and Caledonian companies. The outer positions remained blank, no doubt in anticipation of the Newcastle & Carlisle and Maryport & Carlisle coming into the fold.

A nine bay office section to the right of the clock tower was characterised by little wooden dormer windows peeping above the parapet. Further out, there were ancillary wings, one single-storied, the other with an oriel window. Robust chimneys in groups of six completed the fine facade. Dressed cream stone was used throughout, complementing the city walls and Smirke's Citadel lawcourts. The interior was just as lavish, notably the lofty refreshment room with its huge neo-Tudor fireplace. Needless to say, such extravagant architecture did not come cheap - by 1850 nearly £200,000 had been spent on the station, most of it coming from the Lancaster & Carlisle. Having recovered from near bankruptcy brought about by its wayward expansion policy, the Caledonian finally paid its fair share four years later.

Following the protracted disputes surrounding its genesis, Citadel experienced a calm spell as West Coast traffic consolidated. Nevertheless, another source of strife was looming. The Glasgow & South Western was reluctantly admitted to Citadel in March 1851, heralding a long-running feud. As far as some drivers were concerned, this even continued after the LMS was formed in 1923! Having eaten humble pie, the Maryport & Carlisle was accommodated at the joint station from June 1851. A dedicated bay was provided at the south end of the down platform, but the Lancaster & Carlisle and Caledonian made sure the West Cumberland company knew its place. In fact Citadel was thoroughly dominated by its proprietors, despite having two tenants. West Coast expresses made extended refreshment stops there and the English partner opened the *County Hotel* in 1853.

On 10th May 1857 the Citadel Station Committee was formed. It had four directors from each partner and functioned more or less as a separate railway company. In October 1861 the Committee was forced to admit the North British to Citadel, having lost a long legal battle to keep the Edinburgh company at bay. The Newcastle & Carlisle had also been attempting to gain entry on favourable terms, but was often distracted by aggressive takeover bids from the North Eastern Railway.

To its credit, the Citadel Committee had already taken steps to cater for the inevitable upsurge in traffic. The Act of 22nd July 1861 gave the go-ahead for enlargement of the station and the construction of separate goods lines round the western side (Chapter 10). It also formalised the status of the Committee and confirmed tenancy agreements with the G&SW, Maryport and North British companies, By this time the English partner was the formidable LNWR. Having finally acquired the Newcastle & Carlisle in 1862, the powerful North Eastern soon reached an agreement with the Committee and passenger services were transferred from London Road in January 1863.

By this time the enlargements had been completed at a cost of almost £40,000. Under the existing (but lengthened) overall roof the layout was changed completely. The western or down platform was removed and replaced by carriage sidings, whilst the former up platform was widened and extended. Crossovers were installed so that two trains could be dealt with at the same time. Two north-facing and three south-facing bays were provided for Citadel's tenants (G&SW/North British and Maryport & Carlisle/North Eastern respectively). Meanwhile, Carlisle was becoming a true railway city. Dentonholme, beyond the River Caldew, housed increasing numbers of railwaymen rather than textile workers, for instance.

By the mid-1860s it was clear that the LNWR/Caledonian stranglehold on Citadel could not last. Midland carriages were already a familiar sight at Carlisle and the Settle & Carlisle project was about to get underway. As construction work in the high Pennines progressed, the Committee was required to address the inadequacies of the joint station once again. By the end of the decade it was obvious that the single through platform would become a complete bottleneck when the proposed new Anglo-Scottish alliance materialised.

Although only a tenant of Citadel, the North British promoted a Bill to enlarge the station in 1871, but this astonishing move was rejected by Parliament. The LNWR and Caledonian attempted a similar move during 1872, but this proposal was thrown out because of technicalities associated with the Settle & Carlisle Act. In characteristic fashion, the enterprising Midland board decided to sort matters out itself and came up with a plan which was accepted by the joint proprietors in December 1872. This led to the Citadel Station Act of 21st July 1873, sanctioning reconstruction on a large scale. However, the Midland had to pay out a fair amount of cash as its part of the bargain. New goods lines, well away from the station, were an integral part of the improvement (Chapter 10) and work on the passenger facilities could not begin until these had been completed. They finally opened in 1877, by which time trains had started to run over the Settle & Carlisle line, resulting in the predicted congestion at Citadel. Transformation of the station finally commenced in October 1878.

In its new guise the station occupied 10 acres, the platforms alone covering no less than $2\frac{1}{4}$ acres. The existing through platform was realigned and extended yet again, whilst a new island platform with a bay at its southern end for Maryport & Carlisle trains was built on the site of the former goods lines. Dominating the third version of Citadel was a massive overall roof, 1,030 ft long and 240 ft wide. It consisted of 26 deep lattice girders, approximately 40ft apart, supporting a series of cantilever beams. The glazing, proudly, was to 'Randel's Patent Indestructible System'! From a distance it appeared rather box-like and the lack of smoke vents meant that the glass soon became coated with soot. However, the deep end-screens were truly remarkable. They were boldly executed in an intricate

A fine prospect of the southern approach to Carlisle station on 23rd July 1952. The new and old No.5 signal cabins can be seen in front of the bulk of Citadel at the centre of this view. An 0-6-0T shunts Bog yard on the left and Crown Street depot to the right is well filled with wagons. The Maryport & Carlisle alignment is in the left foreground, the former LNWR main line is nearest the camera, and the connection to London Road used by Newcastle and Settle & Carlisle trains falls away to the right.

On the cold and cloudy morning of 6th April 1963, Ivatt 4MT Mogul No.43045 rolls into platform 4 at Citadel with the 10.48am branch train from Langholm, bringing Saturday shoppers for an afternoon in the Border City. Photograph W.A.C. Smith.

Tudor-Gothic style to blend with Tite's main building - and did so admirably.

There was a proliferation of booking offices at Citadel, reflecting its role as the meeting point of seven companies. In the entrance hall, windows for the LNWR and Caledonian defiantly faced those selling tickets for the Midland, North British and G&SW. The North Eastern had its own office, whilst buildings on the island platform incorporated separate facilities for the three Scottish companies at the northern end and a Maryport & Carlisle window near that company's bay. Fortunately, the refreshment rooms, parcels offices and other amenities essential at a large station were under the control of the Joint Committee. Two wide footbridges connected the main up platform with the island platform and hoists served a luggage/parcels subway beneath the tracks. At the north end of the island platform a ramp descended from Victoria Viaduct, which had replaced a road underbridge shortly before the station was rebuilt.

As construction work on Citadel proceeded, one date was regarded with some trepidation by the Committee - 10th July 1880. This was to be the commencement of the Royal Agricultural Show, destined for Carlisle that year. A massive programme of excursion trains was planned and tens of thousands of visitors were expected. Fortunately, the island platform was completed on 4th July, just in time for the influx. This was just as well, for the final day of the show saw no less then 58 extras in addition to 69 ordinary services. However, passengers had to make their way along unsurfaced platforms and there was no roof. In fact the huge project was not fully completed until July 1881. By then, nearly £500,000 had been spent on the goods lines, approach tracks and the station itself.

Citadel was controlled by LNWR signalling equipment, the semaphores and cabins being similar to those all the way along the main line from Euston. Carlisle No.5, just south of the station, had 114 levers and at busy periods changed a signal or point every minute. No.4, at the northern end, had 56 levers. An intermediate cabin with 40 levers, No.4A, controlled crossovers dividing the platform roads. It was situated on the first floor of the island platform buildings and blended perfectly with their Tudor styling.

Services from each of the eight platforms were fairly well defined, although the numbering system must have confused newcomers and casual travellers. No.5 Main was the up through platform nearest the entrance from Court Square and handled southbound expresses as well as LNWR trains starting at Carlisle. No.2 Main, the inner side of the island platform, was used by up and down Midland/North British/G&SW through workings as well as various Scottish services commencing at Carlisle. Down West Coast expresses and terminating LNWR services used No.1 Main, the outer edge of the island.

A pattern of Anglo-Scottish services calling at the rebuilt Citadel soon emerged and this persisted until fairly recent times. There were three distinct groups. From noon to about 2.00pm several up West Coast expresses called at No.5 Main, including one for Liverpool and Manchester. Meanwhile, a couple of down West Coast services paused at No.1 Main and both up and down Midland services used No.2 Main. There was a similar sequence in mid to late afternoon. Carlisle was at its busiest as far as expresses were concerned from midnight through the small hours. Up to four West Coast and three Midland northbound sleepers were followed by a succession of down trains which often continued until 6am.

The four bays incorporated in No.5 Main had specific uses, although two of them bore the same numbers as the island through platforms! No.1 was used by Midland local traffic and certain North Eastern and LNWR services while No.2

handled North Eastern trains almost exclusively. At the north end, Nos.3 and 4 saw North British workings to Silloth, Langholm and over the Waverley route. No.5 bay, at the south end of the island, was Maryport & Carlisle territory. Local services came and went at frequent intervals from 6.00am to 11.00pm.

Day to day activity at Citadel was impressive enough, but there were also plenty of special occasions. Excited crowds watched the lightning changes of engines during the races to Edinburgh in 1888 and Aberdeen in 1895, for example. Queen Victoria paused at the Border City four times a year on her way to and from Balmoral and her guests included most Crowned Heads of Europe.

As the 19th century drew to a close, there was a significant improvement at Citadel. In 1899 electric lighting in the form of 63 arc lamps and 700 incandescent bulbs replaced the original gas mantles. Unfortunately, there was something more fundamental which needed improving, but it was never tackled. At the height of summer, Carlisle station became a byword for congestion. Midland expresses had to cut across the path of West Coast trains, an enormous amount of marshalling of coaches was necessary, and seasonal extras tended to come in batches. It was not unusual for several northbound services to be held up outside the station when no up trains were in sight. Despite the scissors crossings, three through platforms were inadequate and it is surprising that the carriage sidings on the west side were not sacrificed for more platform accommodation.

Carlisle developed into one of the greatest railway centres in the world during the early 1900s. There were thousands of employees and top of the list was the Joint Committee Superintendent, William Haythornthwaite. He was described in a contemporary *Railway Magazine* article as a 'benevolent despot, the very epitome of railway efficiency, who conveyed an air of great placidity until roused'. Mr. Haythornthwaite governed Citadel in a stern and impartial manner, insisting on co-operation rather than conflict between the seven companies. His day and night stationmasters, together with their staff of inspectors, kept the place running as smoothly as possible.

Although Carlisle was hardly a tourist centre in those days, it became an irresistible draw for Edwardian railway enthusiasts. The Anglo-Scottish expresses were the centre of attention, but express fish traffic, the Stranraer boat trains, special 'horse and carriage' workings (loading up to twenty vehicles) and local services scurrying off in all directions were keenly observed by eager visitors. The succession of overnight sleepers heading north prior to the 'Feast of St. Grouse' on 12th August generated considerable excitement. Carlisle saw even more activity during World War I, particularly on the goods side, but the mood was sombre and most young observers had gone on active service.

With the grouping of 1923, Citadel became the preserve of just two companies - the LMS and LNER. Apart from letting out the *County Hotel* to a private operator, the Station Committee carried on much as before and little was done to the bricks and mortar. Rather, the most noticeable changes involved motive power, new designs mingling with well known locomotives from pre-grouping years. On Friday 29th July 1932, a gentleman by the name of J.C. Mathewson spent the afternoon at Carlisle recording arrivals and departures between noon and 6pm. The following account has been compiled from his hitherto unpublished notes, with additional material by W.A.C. Smith.

'Summer 1932 had brought substantial accelerations to the LMS main line, workings being monopolised by the relatively new Royal Scot 4-6-0s. Even these required assistance on their namesake train however, the up working loading to sixteen vehicles and the down service to no less than seventeen on this occasion. Engines were

Platform 1, the outer edge of the island, looked particularly bleak after the overall roof was removed. On 3rd August 1963, Holbeck A1 Pacific No.60146 PEREGRINE has several admirers as it takes water prior to heading into Scotland. Kingmoor Clan No.72008 CLAN MACLEOD and a Birmingham RCW Type 2 diesel stand back, as if to pay homage. The gaunt wall which once supported the train shed forms a backdrop. Photograph P.B. Booth, Neville Stead Collection.

Class 6MT Pacific No.72008 CLAN MACLEOD pulls out of platform 5 with the 16.37 local over the Settle & Carlisle to Bradford Forster Square, on 7th August 1965. Removal of the overall roof at the southern end transformed this end of the station into a rather exposed place. Photograph W.A.C. Smith.

changed at Kingmoor or No.12 box as appropriate, there being no booked call at Citadel. Up and down pilots were ex-LNWR Precursor 4-4-0s No.5236 WATT and No.5240 FRIAR respectively.

Former LNWR motive power was surprisingly well represented. Claughton 4-6-0 No.5912 LORD FABER took over the up 'Thames-Forth Express' from A3 Pacific No.2749 FLAMINGO, whilst sister engine No.5928 CHARLES H. DENT replaced Pickersgill 4-6-0 No.14652 on an Aberdeen - Euston train comprising fourteen bogies and two vans. The only other ex-Caledonian loco noted was McIntosh 4-4-0 No.14450, on seven coaches from Edinburgh Princes Street.

No.5976 came in with the morning train from Liverpool and Manchester which was taken forward to Glasgow Central by Royal Scot No.6128 METEOR. Another ex-LNWR engine, No.6005, piloted Royal Scot 6107 ARGYLL & SUTHERLAND HIGHLANDER on the Edinburgh portion of the down 'Royal Scot' which ran as a separate train. Claughton No.5932 SIR THOMAS WILLIAMS arrived with the northbound 'Thames-Forth Express', being replaced at Carlisle by A3 4-6-2 No.2749 FLAMINGO. Then the thirteen-coach 'Thames-Clyde Express' was brought in by reboilered Claughton No.5953 BUCKINGHAM piloted by Precursor No.5273 JASON, a Royal Scot taking over for the journey north.

Another Royal Scot replaced No.5910 J.A. BRIGHT on a Euston - Glasgow/Edinburgh express, followed by No.5906 RALPH BROCKLEBANK on a down fitted freight consisting of fifty vans. Ex-LNWR Prince of Wales 4-6-0 No.5733 was one of the station pilots, whilst Precedent 2-4-0s Nos.5001 SNOWDEN and 5032 THE QUEEN, together with Precursor 4-4-2T No.5833, left with Whitehaven trains composed of six-wheel stock. A combined Birmingham/Liverpool/Manchester train was brought in by L&Y type 4-6-0 No.10453, this being replaced by LMS Compound 4-4-0 No.920 for the run to Glasgow.

Time keeping was of a high order, with only two offenders. The up 'Thames - Clyde Express' left five minutes late, ex-Midland 2P 4-4-0s Nos.536 and 540 having replaced Royal Scot No.6154 THE HUSSAR. A fifteen coach train from Glasgow to Liverpool, Manchester, Birmingham and Bournemouth departed ten minutes late behind Royal Scot No.6130 LIVERPOOL which had replaced another member of the class, No.6121 H.L.I. (its actual name).

On the LNER side, ex-North British Atlantic, No.9876 WAVERLEY worked an Edinburgh Waverley train, steam railcar No.35 NETTLE left for Langholm, and Newcastle trains were brought in by D20 4-4-0s No.2011 and 2012 and D29 4-4-0 No.9360 GUY MANNERING.'

Shortly afterwards, the mighty Stanier Pacifics became a familiar sight on West Coast expresses but the fabric of Citadel and its approaches received little attention. In 1938 barriers and booths were installed creating a 'closed' station, whilst the southern footbridge was removed during the dark days of World War II.

As the blackouts and congestion associated with the hostilities faded into history, Carlisle became a railway frontier once again. Nationalisation of the system in 1948 meant that the Border City functioned as the major 'frontier' between BR's Scottish and London Midland Regions. The state-owned giant decided that Citadel badly needed a lot of money spent on it, but so did a lot of other places. At least a start was made. No.5 signal box, on the east side of the main line just south of the station, was replaced by a modern cabin on the west side of the tracks during 1951. No.6 box, where the Maryport line diverged, was also affected by this development, although it continued to function in a minor role until 1953. A particularly welcome development, so far as passengers were concerned, was a complete renumbering of the platforms, logically, from west to east. The island faces became Nos 1 and 3, with the Maryport & Carlisle bay being designated No.2. Up expresses were accommodated at No.4 (the former No.5 main) whilst the four bays for local traffic became Nos 5 to 8.

Departures from Carlisle Citadel for Scottish destinations, Monday to Saturday, Summer 1958.

MO - Mondays Only
MX - Mondays Excepted
MSO - Mondays and Saturdays only
MSX - Mondays and Saturday excepted
FO - Fridays only
FX - Fridays Excepted
FSO - Fridays and Saturdays only
SO - Saturdays only
SX - Saturdays excepted
TC - Through coaches
RC - Restaurant Car
RB - Restaurant Buffet
SC - Sleeping Coaches

1.13am	SO Newcastle - Stranraer Harbour
2.37am	London Euston - Stranraer Harbour THE NORTHERN IRISHMAN SC
3.16am	Ayr (via Kilmarnock)
4.11am	SO London St. Pancras - Glasgow St. Enoch
4.12am	Birmingham New Street - Glasgow Central SC / Edinburgh Princes Street
4.23am	MSO Manchester Exchange - Glasgow Central SC
4.40am	London Euston - Glasgow Central - (SC Euston - Motherwell and Rugby - Glasgow, TC Penzance - Glasgow)
4.43am	SO Nottingham Midland - Edinburgh Waverley
4.55am	SO London St. Pancras - Glasgow St. Enoch
5.01am	SX London St. Pancras - Edinburgh Waverley SC
5.04am	MSX Manchester Exchange / Liverpool Lime Street - Glasgow Central / Edinburgh Princes St. SC
5.10am	SO London St. Pancras - Edinburgh Waverley SC
5.30am	SO London St. Pancras - Glasgow St. Enoch SC
5.36am	SX London Euston - Perth SC
5.41am	SX London St. Pancras - Glasgow St. Enoch SC
5.41am	SO London Euston - Perth SC
6.30am	London Euston - Glasgow St. Enoch SC, RC from Carlisle
7.00am	Glasgow St. Enoch
7.15am	London Euston - Glasgow Central SC, also RC from Carlisle
7.45am	Glasgow St. Enoch
9.00am	Glasgow Central (all stations)
9.05am	Edinburgh Waverley
9.54am	SO Newcastle - Heads of Ayr
11.08am	Glasgow St. Enoch
11.13am	SO Morecambe Euston Road - Glasgow Central
11.27am	SX Manchester Victoria - Glasgow Central RC (TC Edinburgh Princes Street)
11.38am	SX Liverpool Exchange - Glasgow Central RC (TC Edinburgh Princes Street)
12.00	SO Blackpool Central - Glasgow Central
12.13pm	SO Leeds City - Gourock
12.24pm	SO Liverpool Exchange / Southport Chapel Street - Glasgow Central
12.36pm	SO Manchester Victoria - Glasgow Central RC (TC Edinburgh Princes Street)
12.43pm	SX London Euston - Glasgow Central THE CALEDONIAN RC
12.47pm	SO Liverpool Exchange - Glasgow Central RC (TC Edinburgh Princes Street)
1.00pm	SO Manchester Victoria - Glasgow Central (via Kilmarnock)
1.19pm	Leeds City - Glasgow St. Enoch (RC to Kilmarnock)
1.28pm	SX Edinburgh Waverley
1.33pm	SO Lancaster Castle - Glasgow Central
1.36pm	SO Birmingham New Street / Sheffield Midland - Glasgow St. Enoch
1.45pm	SX Manchester Victoria - Aberdeen (RC to Perth and TC Crewe - Perth)
1.45pm	SO Edinburgh Waverley
1.48pm	SO Crewe - Aberdeen
1.56pm	SO Blackpool Central - Perth RC (TC Aberdeen and Edinburgh Princes Street)
2.33pm	Stranraer Harbour (TC from Newcastle FSO)
3.22pm	SX Galashiels
3.30pm	SO Edinburgh Waverley
3.43pm	SX Birmingham New Street - Glasgow Central RC
3.54pm	SX Birmingham New Street - Edinburgh Princes St. RC
4.02pm	SO Birmingham New Street - Glasgow Central RC
4.10pm	SX London St. Pancras - Edinburgh Waverley THE WAVERLEY RC
4.15pm	SX London Euston - Glasgow Central / Aberdeen (train divided at Carlisle, Aberdeen portion departing 4.26pm)
4.21pm	SO Birmingham New Street - Edinburgh Princes St. RC
4.30pm	SO London Euston - Glasgow Central RC
4.35pm	SO London St. Pancras - Edinburgh Waverley THE WAVERLEY RC
4.40pm	SO London Euston - Perth RC / Aberdeen
4.52pm	SO London St. Pancras - Glasgow St. Enoch RB
5.05pm	SX London St. Pancras - Glasgow St. Enoch THE THAMES -CLYDE EXPRESS RC
5.05pm	SO Blackpool North - Glasgow Central
5.08pm	Langholm
5.12pm	SO London St. Pancras - Glasgow St. Enoch THE THAMES - CLYDE EXPRESS RC
5.20pm	SX Manchester Victoria / Liverpool Exchange - Glasgow Central / Edinburgh Princes Street
5.20pm	SO Liverpool Exchange - Glasgow Central
5.41pm	SO Manchester Victoria - Glasgow Central / Edinburgh Princes Street

Otherwise, the mighty edifice was little different from late Victorian times, albeit somewhat grubbier. The motive power had changed out of all recognition of course, and if Mr. Mathewson visited Citadel in the early 1950s he would have seen very few of the classes recorded just a couple of decades earlier. W.A.C. Smith took a day trip to Carlisle on Wednesday 1st September 1954. There were plenty of Stanier Pacifics about, but these observations concentrate on the less glamorous workings.

'The journey to Carlisle was aboard the crowded eleven-coach 10.05am departure from Edinburgh Waverley hauled by A3 Pacific No.60101 CICERO. This was the 'Waverley' express for St. Pancras which had been banked out of Hawick by J36 No.65316 as passengers enjoyed a glorious prospect of the sun-dappled hills on the climb to Whitrope. After a punctual 12.44pm arrival at Citadel's platform 4, CICERO came off and was replaced by Jubilee No.45659 DRAKE piloted by Class 5 No.45081 for the climb to Ais Gill.

Class 3F 0-6-0 No.43678 was the north end station pilot, its opposite number being 0-6-0T No.47556. Jubilee No.45717 DAUNTLESS soon came into platform 1, some 20 minutes late, with the 9.30am Manchester Victoria - Glasgow Central, due at 12.28pm. At the south end, B1 No.61238 LESLIE RUNCIMAN left from platform 6 with the 1.05pm to Newcastle. The 9.00am from Perth to Euston arrived at platform 3 at 1.10pm, 22 minutes late, behind Class 5 No.44701. Coronation Pacific No.46253 CITY OF ST. ALBANS took over, but another minute had been lost. Timekeeping was not good. Class 5 No.44787 ran into platform 4 with the 10.40am Glasgow Central - Liverpool Lime Street, due at 1.06pm, and was replaced by No.45306. At least the 1.25pm to Whitehaven hauled by Fowler 2-6-4T No.42428 left on time.

A trip on the Langholm branch followed. A3 Pacific No.60095 FLAMINGO, a long standing resident of Canal shed, was in charge of six coaches and two vans forming the 1.26pm semi-fast to Edinburgh Waverley, and this train provided transport as far as Riddings Junction. On the opposite side of the island platform J39 No.64884 waited with the 2.00pm to Langholm. The same engine worked the 3.28pm from Langholm to Carlisle. This drew into the north end of platform 4 behind the 1.45pm from Glasgow Central to Liverpool and Manchester, hauled by a Clan Pacific.

Shortly afterwards, Britannia Pacific, No.70051 (new out of Crewe Works and as yet to be named FIRTH OF FORTH) left with the 10.10am from Euston to Glasgow Central. The down 'Waverley' (9.00am St. Pancras to Edinburgh) rolled into platform 3, four minutes early at 4.25pm, hauled by Standard

(continued from overleaf)

5.54pm	Glasgow St. Enoch
6.13pm	SX Hawick
6.55pm	FO Plymouth North Road / Crewe - Glasgow Central
7.10pm	SX London Euston - Glasgow Central THE MID-DAY SCOT RC (TC Plymouth North Road - Glasgow Central FX)
7.25pm	SO London Euston - Glasgow Central - THE MID-DAY SCOT RC
7.36pm	SX Manchester Exchange / Liverpool Exchange - Glasgow Central / Edinburgh Princes St.
7.40pm	SO Manchester Exchange / Liverpool Exchange - Glasgow Central RC / Edinburgh Princes St.
7.44pm	Edinburgh Waverley
7.50pm	Glasgow St. Enoch
8.27pm	London Euston - Perth RC
8.30pm	SO Langholm
9.08pm	SX London Euston - Glasgow Central THE CALEDONIAN RC
9.19pm	SO Hawick

Departures from Carlisle Citadel for English destinations, Monday to Saturday, Summer 1960

12.10am	Glasgow Central - London Euston SC
12.22am	MO Glasgow Central - London Euston SC
12.30am	MX Oban & Glasgow Central - London Euston SC
12.48am	SO Stranraer Harbour - Newcastle
12.54am	Perth - London Euston SC
12.59am	Edinburgh Waverley - London St. Pancras SC
1.30am	MX Stranraer Harbour - London Euston THE NORTHERN IRISHMAN SC
1.41am	Inverness - London Euston THE ROYAL HIGHLANDER SC
1.52am	Glasgow Central / Edinburgh Princes Street - Birmingham New St SC)
2.20am	Glasgow Central - Liverpool Lime St SC (also TC Edinburgh Princes St. - Manchester Exchange)
2.32am	Glasgow Central - Manchester Exchange (via Hellifield) SC & TC
2.50am	Newcastle
5.45am	Whitehaven Bransty
6.10am	Carlisle - Euston (RC Crewe - Euston)
6.45am	Silloth
6.55am	Newcastle
7.05am	Whitehaven Bransty
7.35am	Newcastle
8.05am	Hellifield (all stations)
8.25am	Whitehaven Bransty
8.40am	Carlisle - London Euston RC (also TC from Windermere)
9.00am	Newcastle
9.10am	Silloth
9.25am	Whitehaven Bransty
9.52am	Workington Main (via Penrith & Keswick)
10.19am	Glasgow Central - London Euston THE CALEDONIAN RC
10.35am	Whitehaven Bransty
10.40am	SO Newcastle (16th July - 20th August)
11.02am	Newcastle
11.10am	Workington Main (via Penrith & Keswick)
11.20am	Silloth
11.20am	SO Ayr - Liverpool Exchange / Manchester Victoria (via Hellifield)
11.25am	Whitehaven Bransty
11.29am	SO Heads of Ayr - Leeds City
11.47am	MFSO Glasgow St. Enoch - London St. Pancras
12.07pm	Glasgow St. Enoch - London St. Pancras THE THAMES-CLYDE EXPRESS RC
12.19pm	Edinburgh Princes Street - Birmingham New Street RC
12.25pm	Whitehaven Bransty
12.29pm	Glasgow Central - Birmingham New Street RC (TC Plymouth FX)
12.39pm	Glasgow Central - London Euston RC (TC Plymouth FO)
12.42pm	FO Sheffield Midland (22nd July - 13th August)
12.42pm	SO Edinburgh Waverley - Sheffield Midland
12.57pm	Perth - London Euston RC
12.58pm	Edinburgh Waverley - London St. Pancras THE WAVERLEY RC
1.00pm	Newcastle
1.00pm	SO Whitehaven Bransty
1.14pm	Glasgow Central / Edinburgh Princes Street - Liverpool Exchange RC
1.16pm	Silloth
1.23pm	Glasgow Central - Manchester Victoria RC
1.25pm	SX Whitehaven Bransty
1.40pm	SO Silloth
1.47pm	Aberdeen / Dundee West / Edinburgh Princes Street - Manchester Victoria RC
1.50pm	SO Whitehaven Bransty
2.20pm	Newcastle
2.25pm	Whitehaven Bransty
2.40pm	Newcastle
3.04pm	Glasgow Central - London Euston THE MID-DAY SCOT RC
3.22pm	SO Newcastle
3.25pm	Whitehaven Bransty
3.25pm	Silloth
3.59pm	Aberdeen - London Euston RC
4.13pm	Glasgow Central / Edinburgh Princes Street - Manchester Victoria / Liverpool Exchange
4.20pm	Newcastle
4.25pm	Whitehaven Bransty
4.37pm	Bradford Forster Square (all stations)
4.42pm	SO Silloth

Class 5 No.73053. CICERO was late off Canal shed and the train departed at 4.43pm instead of 4.37pm. J39 No.64727 was on the 4.48pm to Silloth at platform 8, Ivatt 2MT mogul No.46491 headed the 4.58pm to Keswick at the south end of platform 4, sister engine No.46458 was in charge of the 5.08pm to Whitehaven at platform 2 and B1 No.61219 backed on to the 5.20pm for Newcastle at platform 6.

Royal Scot No.46117 WELSH GUARDSMAN came into platform 3 one minute early with the down 'Thames-Clyde Express' and No.46102 BLACK WATCH paused at platform 1 with a down Liverpool / Manchester - Glasgow Central train. The 1.53pm 'Parly' from Glasgow Central, calling at all 27 stations en route and taking 3 hours 27 minutes, arrived behind Jubilee No.45600 BERMUDA, while the corresponding 2.00pm from St. Enoch was pulled by No.45707 VALIANT. The 2.33pm from Edinburgh then arrived with B1 No.61395 in charge.

Compound No.40913 worked the 5.51pm local over the Sou'West line, comprising nine coaches and a gas cylinder wagon, and No.41146 ran through from the north with a milk train. Other observations were 2P No.40652 on an arrival from Whitehaven, No.40615 on the 5.57 to Appleby and 2MT No.46455 on the 6.10pm to Penrith. The last was a little disappointing as the train was often worked by one of the few remaining LNWR 'Cauliflower' 0-6-0s.

D49 No.62732 DUMFRIES-SHIRE headed the 6.13pm to Riccarton Junction, J39 No.64895 came in from Silloth, B1 4-6-0s Nos. 61013 TOPI and 61222 departed on Newcastle trains and the 4.00pm Glasgow St. Enoch to Leeds City was brought in on time by No.46112 SHERWOOD FORESTER. Finally, the 4.05pm Glasgow Central to Liverpool and Manchester arrived behind No.72001 CLAN CAMERON.

The homeward journey was by 'The Midday Scot' 1.30pm off Euston, which arrived slightly ahead of schedule behind immaculate 8P Pacific No.71000 DUKE OF GLOUCESTER, a regular working for the loco at the time. The train consisted of sixteen vehicles, including an ex-GWR through coach from Plymouth.'

By the mid-1950s, Citadel's overall roof was decaying badly, the inevitable outcome of years of deferred maintenance. A decision was taken to demolish the magnificent Victorian end screens and refurbish the train shed as far as possible. Most of the work took place during 1957. The roof over platform 1 and the carriage sidings was removed completely, whilst the remainder was cut back at either end. New end screens of a somewhat excessively functional appearance were erected and exposed stretches of platform acquired steel-framed umbrella canopies. The massive screen walls which supported the roof were retained, a gaunt reminder of the great days.

During the early 1970s preparatory work for electrification swept away much that was familiar, the whole steam age gallimaufry of equipment and buildings in and around Citadel. During 1973 a new power box was built on part of the former Bog Yard. It controlled the six remaining radial routes as far as Annan, Kirkpatrick, Wetheral, Cumwhinton, Oxenholme and Wigton, resulting in the closure and demolition of numerous manual boxes. The once vital scissors crossings in the station were removed at the same time. Masts and overhead for the commencement of electric services in 1974 transformed many traditional views around Citadel.

Pressure cleaning of the station frontage started in 1978 and the former carriage sidings replaced Kingmoor as a loco stabling point a couple of years later. Carlisle became an 'open' station once again in 1984 and television information screens were installed. During 1986 the centre roads were resignalled for reversible freight working, following closure of the goods avoiding lines and a new travel centre was created within the listed main building. Thus, the Citadel familiar to travellers today had evolved - a mixture of ancient and modern with a glorious past and hopefully a bright future.

Above. **The mighty supporting wall enriched with blind Tudor arches at the south end of Citadel served no useful purpose (other than that of wind break) when the roof was cut back. At least it provides a background in this view of Britannia Pacific No.70038 ROBIN HOOD, departing from platform 4 with the 14.00 from Glasgow Central to Liverpool and Manchester, on 22nd July 1967. Photograph W.A.C. Smith**

Below. **Holbeck Jubilee No.45562 ALBERTA (together with No.45593 KOLHAPUR) was a familiar sight at Citadel on summer Saturdays during the final years of steam. However it was a bleak winter day, 25th February 1967, on this occasion. The loco waited at the windswept south end to take over the return leg of a railtour from Leeds. Photograph W.A.C. Smith.**

(Contiued from previous page)	
4.47pm	*SX Silloth*
5.05pm	*Keswick (via Penrith)*
5.15pm	*Whitehaven Bransty*
5.25pm	*Newcastle*
5.52pm	*SO Stranraer Harbour - Newcastle (9th July - 13th August)*
6.05pm	*Appleby West (all stations)*
6.15pm	*Whitehaven Bransty*
6.20pm	*Silloth*
6.56pm	*Glasgow St. Enoch - Leeds City RC*
6.56pm	*Glasgow Central / Edinburgh Princes Street - Manchester Victoria / Liverpool Exchange RC*
7.00pm	*Newcastle*
7.02pm	*Warrington Bank Quay*
7.05pm	*SO Appleby West (all stations)*
7.50pm	*Whitehaven Bransty*
7.55pm	*Workington Main (via Penrith and Keswick)*
8.40pm	*Whitehaven Bransty*
9.00pm	*SX Silloth*
9.00pm	*Newcastle*
9.05pm	*SO Silloth*
9.24pm	*Glasgow Central - London Euston (SC from Carlisle) TC Penzance (SX)*
9.34pm	*FO Glasgow Central - Plymouth*
9.40pm	*Whitehaven Bransty*
10.50pm	*SO Silloth*
11.10pm	*SO Whitehaven Bransty*
11.24pm	*FO Glasgow Central - London Euston*
11.45pm	*FO Glasgow St. Enoch - London St. Pancras*
11.58pm	*Glasgow St. Enoch - London St. Pancras SC*

Above. A fine panorama of Upperby yard on 9th June 1962. Despite the presence of a diesel shunter, this view epitomises the century-old method of dealing with goods traffic in Carlisle. Ex-North British J36 0-6-0 No.65321 is dealing with a trip working from Canal. Photograph G.M. Staddon, Neville Stead Collection.

Below. Part of the Upperby yard complex around 1948-49. A 3F 0-6-0T, possibly No.47618, shunts the sidings. Note the early signal cabin and the odd two-storey building to the left of it.

Chapter 10
GOODS TRAFFIC

The sheer volume of freight traffic passing through Carlisle from the 1860s to the 1960s was astonishing and at certain times it reached paralysing proportions. During the Second World War, for instance, the crew of one particular goods completed a seven hour shift having moved their train just *two miles* across the city, such was the congestion. Carlisle has always been a relatively small place with a limited manufacturing base, but its very location on the national railway network meant that traffic flows converged on the Solway lowlands from north, south, east and west.

With much heavy industry concentrated in Western Scotland and North West England, the exchange of raw materials, components and finished products inevitably involved the West Coast main line. Furthermore, there was London's insatiable demand for all manner of commodities, including those produced in Scotland. Then there were exports through the ports of Liverpool and Glasgow, as well as heavy mineral and steel traffic originating in West Cumberland and North East England.

Unfortunately, the seven pre-grouping companies insisted on maintaining their own yards, despite building joint goods lines and sharing common passenger facilities. Perhaps this was understandable, but the LMS and LNER did little to improve matters, so the complex shunting operations and transfer trips continued much as before. Even BR dragged its heels for a while and when the huge Kingmoor marshalling yard finally opened it was virtually too late. Freight was being lost to road transport at an increasing rate and block trains were about to replace traditional wagon loads.

From July 1836, when the Newcastle & Carlisle reached London Road, to July 1861, when dedicated avoiding lines round the outside of Citadel were authorised, the arrangements for goods traffic at Carlisle were primitive. A series of small depots had opened, but these tended to fulfill specific local needs and the vast increase in business was not anticipated. However, several larger and better equipped yards followed over the ensuing years and the

DIXON'S MILL

Viaduct yard, the Goods Traffic Committee tracks and the northern part of the Dentonholme loop in 1950. A couple of 3F 0-6-0Ts lurk amongst the sea of wagons. Carlisle still had an industrial skyline at the time.

The meagre spell of winter sunshine dies away and shadows lengthen as Black 5 No.44675 passes Upperby shed on 28th November 1964, with a mixed freight for Kingmoor. Photograph W.A.C. Smith.

Carlisle Goods Joint Committee finally put the city's freight workings on a firm footing during the late 1870s.

The Newcastle & Carlisle Railway established a modest goods depot adjacent to its London Road passenger terminus in 1836. This was a useful outlet for the products of local factories and it also received coal for domestic and industrial consumption. Sidings were laid alongside the Carlisle Canal basin when the branch from London Road opened in 1837 - and these even saw some international traffic. As noted in Chapter 2, coal was despatched to Ireland and certain commodities from northern Europe passed this way.

In keeping with its chaotic beginnings, the Maryport & Carlisle used no less than four Carlisle stations for goods traffic between 1843 and 1852. A siding or two at Bog sufficed until 1844, when the doomed Crown Street terminus opened. When this station was ignominiously dismantled in 1849, the Newcastle & Carlisle yard at London Road came to the rescue. Eventually, a purpose-built depot opened on the west side of the Lancaster & Carlisle tracks in January 1852. This was generally known as Crown Street - not to be confused with the ill-fated terminus on the opposite side of the main line, or for that matter the later LNWR yard which occupied its site. Just to confound things further, the permanent Maryport facilities were officially known as Bog from 1924 - not to be confused with the 1843 station!

From the outset, both West Coast partners exchanged long distance goods traffic at Carlisle, but they also built their own depots in the city for domestic purposes. The Lancaster & Carlisle had sidings at St. Nicholas, just north of Upperby. A site near the cathedral known as West Walls was chosen by the Caledonian. Together with the adjacent engine shed, the latter caused friction with the church authorities, as will be seen in the next chapter. Glasgow & South Western goods services were also accommodated at West Walls, albeit with a certain amount of tension.

Finally, having purchased the Carlisle Canal and drained it, the Port Carlisle company adapted the former city basin for railway purposes in 1854. This peculiar site, soon to handle Silloth and Waverley route traffic as well, retained quayside coping stones and mooring bollards amid the sidings. Even the main warehouse at Canal yard had originally been used for waterway transhipments.

With the growing number of goods trains and the imminent arrival of the North British from Edinburgh, badly needed improvements were put in hand. As noted in Chapter 9, the Act of 22nd July 1861 strengthened the powers of the Citadel Station Committee and formalised access to the station by other companies. It also authorised goods relief lines on the western side as part of an overall plan to improve facilities. These opened during 1862 and eased the passage of through freights and transfer trips for a decade or so.

Goods traffic continued to increase and a further upsurge was anticipated in view of the G&SW/North British/Midland alliance. As construction work on the Settle & Carlisle progressed, the Midland began to agitate for drastic improvements to the track layout and facilities in Carlisle. Eventually all the parties agreed that far-reaching changes were necessary and the result was the Citadel Station Act of 17th July 1873. The main aims were to separate passenger and goods operations as far as possible and to provide adequate capacity for both.

Citadel itself was enlarged again, as described in the previous chapter, and the goods relief lines were sacrificed for the extension. They were replaced by a completely new alignment through the western suburbs of Carlisle. This began at a point near Bog Junction (where the original Maryport & Carlisle line joined the Canal branch) to Willowholme Junction on the Caledonian Port Carlisle branch (the connection used by Silloth and Waverley route trains). The 1½ miles of track were administered by the Carlisle Goods Traffic Committee, made up of representatives from the LNWR, Caledonian, Glasgow & South Western and Midland. A considerable amount of ancillary

70

trackwork was carried out so that all seven companies had access to the new formation without interfering with passenger traffic. In the north, closure of West Walls depot allowed the Caledonian main line to be moved further east, thus releasing land for a replacement yard (eventually known as Viaduct) with direct connections to the goods tracks. Freights from the Beattock and Dumfries routes reached the latter via a short spur at Caldew Junction. North British traffic came in at Willowholme Junction, no modifications being necessary.

Engineering work on the southern approach was far more extensive. Maryport & Carlisle access to the goods line was straightforward, involving a short spur from Forks Junction to Rome Street Junction. However, the existing passenger approach to Citadel was no longer feasible and the sweeping curve from Currock Junction to Carlisle No.6 signal box had to be built. Modifications to the LNWR system proved more expensive. The main line was moved slightly west for the second time and raised so that it passed above the Canal branch. At the same time, rails were laid from Upperby to meet the Goods Committee tracks end-on near Bog Junction. On the way, this long spur went under the main line adjacent to the Canal branch bridge.

By now the layout south of Citadel had become very complex. Fortunately, the North Eastern and Midland did not add to the confusion - they were able to reach the goods loop via a straightforward connection from the Canal branch at Bog Junction. Most of the new tracks came into operation over a five week period, culminating in the opening of the Goods Committee line on 7th August 1877. Although there was talk of a common yard, agreement could not be reached and the inevitable outcome was an increase in the already notorious trip workings. The situation was further exacerbated when the Midland, North British and G&SW decided to build a new yard at Dentonholme, to lessen dependence on the West Coast alliance. This was reached by a loop off the Goods Committee line, opened on 1st October 1883.

As a result of the Act of 1861, which acknowledged the need for improved facilities, there had been drastic changes in goods arrangements. Some of the original yards were still in use and had expanded, while several new ones had opened. Eventually all seven companies owned sizeable freight facilities in Carlisle, but they were destined to become increasingly outmoded as investment more or less dried up after World War 1.

The North Eastern Railway developed London Road yard on the north side of the Newcastle line. It spread east of the original goods depot and there was plenty of space for sidings - in fact it became the largest yard in Carlisle, both in terms of area and throughput. Especially important were the trains of coal from Durham and Northumberland pits destined for the city's engine sheds. Other traffic included coke for the Workington steel furnaces and steel bound from Teesside to Scotland. Communications between staff at the original Newcastle & Carlisle depot and the far end of the yard nearly three quarters of a mile away always presented difficulties. There were no such problems at the compact Maryport & Carlisle Bog yard, just south of Citadel. The only major change was revised access brought about by the goods line developments of 1877.

Improvements to LNWR goods facilities were as bewildering as those affecting the company's running lines. St. Nicholas depot was originally served by a spur off the west side of the main line, but when the latter was moved west in 1862, access had to be from the Upperby Junction - London Road Junction spur on the east side of the approach tracks. In 1867 a new depot opened at Crown Street, adjacent to Citadel on the site of the forcibly demolished Maryport & Carlisle terminus. The approach to Crown Street crossed the North Eastern curve from London Road on the level until 1877, when it was raised along with the parallel main line. At the same time the goods branch junction was moved towards Upperby.

St. Nicholas yard closed in 1867, but reopened in 1871 as a cattle

Carlisle's goods avoiding lines were often used by seasonal passenger trains not booked to call at Citadel, notably those associated with Glasgow holidays. However, on 28th October 1967 Black 5 No.44767 was hauling the RCTS 'Border Limited' railtour from Crewe as it left the West Coast line at Upperby. A Signal & Telegraph Department coach languishes on the right, whilst Upperby carriage sidings and the shed coaling plant can be seen on the left. Photograph W.A.C. Smith.

An Illustrated History of Carlisle's Railways

With Citadel prominent in the background, former Maryport & Carlisle 0-4-2T No.11563 backs wagons into Bog yard in 1927 shortly before it was withdrawn. The engine was built at Maryport works in 1865 and was numbered 17 prior to grouping.

depot. Nearby, a large yard developed at Upperby for exchange traffic, access being overseen by Upperby Junction (No.12) box. This cabin was one of the busiest in Carlisle; besides controlling the yard entrance it had responsibilities for the main line, the goods tracks to Bog Junction, the spur to London Road, Upperby shed, St. Nicholas cattle dock, the carriage depot and a wagon repair shop. Upperby could be a difficult yard to work, as all goods trains and trips from the north had to pause on the freight departure lines and reverse into the yard when they could be accepted.

When West Walls was abandoned, the Caledonian developed two sites for goods traffic. Sidings were laid on both sides of the main line at Kingmoor, principally for despatching and receiving long distance Scottish traffic. The other was Viaduct yard just north of Citadel, another awkward place to work as traffic increased. Trains from the south had to be drawn forward then backed in when there was room, a process which could take up to fifteen minutes. Once inside, shunting was often interrupted by the arrival and departure of other trains, trips and light engines, for all these had to pass over the shunting neck. Some trains had to be shunted twice as the yard was in two sections with a common exchange siding known as 'Pincher'. When arrivals were bunched, some were sent to Kingmoor, but at really busy periods in the 1950s it was not unusual for freights to be held back at Dentonholme North Box, Rome Street, Bog Junction, Upperby Junction or even loops on the main line.

Having been a tenant at West Walls and other yards in Carlisle, the G&SW embraced Dentonholme as its first proper base in the city for goods traffic. In fact the North British and Midland made little use of the depot, even though they had shared the cost of the loop. Dentonholme eventually became an important reception point for overnight trains from England, as will be outlined later.

Canal yard remained historically interesting because of its origins, but this North British site became a cramped and difficult one to operate, despite a certain amount of expansion. In its final form it consisted of two sections, separated by the tracks from Rome Street Junction. The older part, on the eastern side, was the original basin site, modified on several occasions. The sidings were of various lengths and had strange names like 'Young Kytle' and 'Back and Front Modders'. Unexpected connections added to the general confusion. All traffic via Willowholme Junction had to set back along the Silloth branch or even the Waverley route before reversing into the yard.

The Midland established a warehouse and yard at Petterill (officially *Petteril* Bridge from 1909) which were ready for the start of goods services over the Settle & Carlisle in 1875. They stood on the south side of the Leeds line within sight of London Road and Upperby depots, in an area becoming dominated by railway business. Sidings were also laid out at Durranhill South and in BR days these became a major departure point for overnight fitted freights to London, Birmingham, Derby, Nottingham, Leicester, Manchester, Bradford and other destinations.

Following grouping, the LMS and LNER were able to rearrange trip workings and introduce more flexibility into the deployment of Carlisle's yards, a process which went further when the whole system was under the control of British Railways. However, the proliferation, location and layout of the depots meant that only so much could be done. Traffic was still very heavy in 1960 and a brief look at goods operations in the Border City just two generations ago illustrates the problems and achievements. It also reveals a system of freight transport which must seen alien to today's youngsters.

Nearly all the yards built by the seven pre-grouping companies were still at work. They had two basic functions: firstly, receiving incoming trains to be made up into trips for other yards; secondly, taking in trips for making up into

Midland Railway staff facilities sometimes fell short of the standards reached by the company's stations and rolling stock! A kettle comes to the boil in a cabin at Durranhill South Sidings in the early 1950s.

72

An Illustrated History of Carlisle's Railways

Black 5 No.45299 passes Bog Junction on the avoiding line from London Road Junction to Rome Street Junction (the former Canal branch) with a northbound goods. Several features of Carlisle's complex southern approaches could be seen on this sunny autumn afternoon, 2nd September 1967. The LNWR goods tracks from Upperby Junction are parallel to the train and the spur from Currock Junction comes in from the right - this was the original Maryport & Carlisle approach to the city. Just beyond Bog Junction box, a girder bridge carries the later Maryport & Carlisle spur from Currock Junction. The main West Coast route is immediately behind the M&C bridge and the Cowans Sheldon crane works is on the left. Photograph W.A.C. Smith.

outgoing trains. The situation was complicated by the running of complete trains to outgoing yards and the specific duties of particular depots - handling sundries traffic and shunting private sidings for example. These activities took place on a system which developed with precious little overall planning.

Trip workings were crucial to the handling of goods traffic. Although these operated in most major railway centres, they became an institution at Carlisle and during the 1950s up to 18 engines a day could be in steam for such duties. Trips came largely into three categories. Firstly, there was the movement of sorted wagons from reception yard to dispatch yard - the most common function. Secondly, locos were allocated specific jobs such as shunting coal depots and private sidings. Thirdly, trip engines often replaced train engines on incoming freights to relieve main line crews of the often lengthy wait for entry into a yard.

Certain trip workings were associated with inter-train connections, but the usual practice was to use engines for 'minute to minute' needs on orders from Control. Relief crews were sent to take over a loco wherever it happened to be at the time. The size of trips varied from a single wagon to a complete train. In early BR days 30,000 wagons a week were exchanged between Carlisle's yard -

it had been 50,000 at the height of World War 1.

Arrivals and departures in 1960 were far too complex to consider in detail here, but an outline will give a flavour of the huge operation. Down trains from the former LNWR main line were mainly received at Viaduct, although a few went to Dentonholme or Kingmoor. Services from the Midland route arrived at London Road, the reception sidings at Petteril Bridge having closed in 1959, but some used Viaduct, Dentonholme, Kingmoor or Canal. London Road also received traffic from the Newcastle and Maryport directions, with the occasional train from the Cumbrian coast terminating in sidings at Currock. Services from Silloth and the Waverley route headed for Canal, whilst those via Beattock and Dumfries arrived at Kingmoor, except for a few overnight fitted freights which went direct to Upperby or Durranhill South.

Departures were more straightforward and normally kept to the following pattern: LNWR line from Upperby; Midland line from Durranhill South; North Eastern line from London Road; Maryport & Carlisle line from London Road and sometimes Currock; North British lines from Canal; Caledonian and G&SW lines from Viaduct and Kingmoor, with a few from Dentonholme or London Road.

For an insight into the actual working of the yards it is worth examining the overnight activity at Dentonholme, as described in *Carlisle-Border Freight Centre*, an article by K.D. Peel in *Trains Illustrated*, July 1961. *'By the time the night shift arrives at 10pm the yard foreman has already received telegraphs concerning train loadings including those of the Class C freights from Liverpool Edge Hill, London Broad Street and Camden, all of which have portions for Scotland with tight schedules to keep.*

The 6.24pm from Edge Hill arrives on the Dentonholme loop first. It is booked to run through to Kingmoor with consignments for the former Caledonian and G&SW routes, but there are wagons for other lines and Carlisle itself at the front. The train engine draws forward, the yard pilot removes those vehicles which require sorting and the main line loco takes the remainder to Kingmoor. Shunting proceeds as the 1.00pm from Broad Street and 2.18pm from Camden reach Carlisle after their long journeys from the south of England. Each has wagons for Carlisle and a variety of other destinations at the front, together with portions for Glasgow Buchanan Street at the rear.

Both trains are broken and the Buchanan Street portions marshalled ready for a Stanier class 5 to take them north at 11.50pm. Meanwhile, a trip en-

73

Ex-LMS 8F 2-8-0 No.48200 passes Bog Junction with wagons of long-welded rails on 16th September 1967. The train has just used the former LNWR tracks from Upperby Junction. Photograph W.A.C. Smith.

gine from Canal shed has arrived. Shortly after the Scottish train departs, it backs on to a string of wagons which have already been shunted and hauls them to Canal yard where they will be attached to the 1.10am for Dundee and 1.35am to Perth. A second trip heads for Kingmoor with vehicles for the 1.47am to Glasgow College and 2.40am for Edinburgh Lothian Road. Although the busiest period is over, there is still a residue of shunting at Dentonholme until dawn'.

Despite the activity at Carlisle's yards in 1960, the whole operation was living on borrowed time. There were ominous signs even before grouping when one-man haulage businesses were set up using surplus military lorries after World

A view north from the bridge near Bog Junction looking towards Rome Street Junction. On 16th September 1967, Black 5 No.45061 heads towards London Road Junction with a train of empty hoppers. The tracks from Upperby Junction are in the left foreground and the erstwhile Maryport & Carlisle spur from Forks Junction and Currock comes in background left. Photograph W.A.C. Smith.

Rome Street Junction looking west on 10th September 1960. Woods at Longsowerby and Carlisle's massive textile factory were in the shadows, but a gap in the clouds allowed sunshine to illuminate a Canal-based J36 plodding towards London Road yard with a trip working of just six wagons. The train is using the original Newcastle & Carlisle branch to Canal basin. On the right, the Goods Committee line heads away towards Dentonholme and Caldew Junction. Photograph J.J. Smith.

War 1. However, it took half a century for road transport to capture the huge amount of railway goods traffic which had grown up and thrived in the Border City. But the process is now virtually complete and even the brave but belated Kingmoor New Yard project never fulfilled expectations.

Early goods closures in the Carlisle area were confined to places where unfavourable circumstances prevailed. The demise of Solway viaduct

Having negotiated the former North Eastern Railway Canal branch and Rome Street Junction, Britannia Pacific No.70013 OLIVER CROMWELL guides a down goods towards Kingmoor yard on 2nd September 1967. Seventeen years later, a portion of this bridge across the River Caldew plunged into the water when runaway freightliner wagons smashed into the girders at high speed. The Carlisle avoiding line was never re-opened. Photograph W.A.C. Smith.

Viaduct yard was below the level of the main line, as can be seen in the background of this view. On 6th April 1963 Fowler 2-6-4T No.42301 pauses at Carlisle No.4 box during shunting operations at Citadel. Photograph W.A.C. Smith.

meant the end of Bowness yard on 1st September 1921, whilst the abandoning of Brampton Town on 1st January 1924 and Port Carlisle on 1st June 1932 came about because of the desire to eliminate branches maintained specifically for these depots. Scotby (ex-Midland) and Wreay (ex-LNWR) finished on 1st February 1942 and 16th August 1943 respectively. The former was very close to the former North Eastern yard and the latter was remote, its traffic easily absorbed by nearby stations.

The first fifteen years of BR control saw a spasmodic withdrawal of goods facilities in Carlisle's hinterland, as follows:

Scotch Dyke (NB): 2nd May 1949
Floriston (Cal) and Rockcliffe (Cal): 17th July 1950
Gretna (Cal) and Gretna (NB): 10th September 1951
Dearham Bridge (M&C): 15th October 1951
Cotehill (Mid): 7th April 1952
Wetheral (NE): 1st April 1955
Drumburgh (NB): 4th July 1955
Rigg (G&SW): 9th January 1956
Calthwaite (LNW): 4th June 1956
Cumwhinton (Mid): 5th November 1956
Curthwaite (M&C): 6th January 1958
How Mill (NE): 5th January 1959
Scotby (NE): 2nd November 1959
Cummersdale (M&C): 6th March 1961

Towards the end of this phase, Kingmoor New Yard had been taking shape. The provision of purpose-built marshalling facilities at Carlisle was given priority in the 1955 Modernisation Plan and parliamentary approval for the £4.5 million project came in 1956. A strip of prime agricultural land 2½ miles long and ¼ mile wide, between the village of Cargo and the main line north of Kingmoor sidings, was acquired. This site appealed to the planners; with associated trackwork it would be able to receive and dispatch goods traffic in both directions without inconveniencing operations on the West Coast main line.

Preliminary earth moving and drainage work began in October 1959 and a year later the first trains of slag from derelict Cleator Moor ironworks in West Cumberland arrived. Eventually, almost 700,000 tons of hardcore was used to form the base of the yard, a hundred wagonloads a day being received at the peak in January 1961. Most of the ballast originated at Sandside Quarry on the former Furness Railway branch from Hincaster Junction, south of Oxenholme. A train ran every day for over a year and they were hauled by a Tebay Austerity 2-8-0 with one or two bankers providing assistance at the rear. Rails for the 56 miles of track at Kingmoor New Yard came mostly from the United Steel plant at Workington.

The up yard, opened on 25th March 1963, consisted of eight reception roads, 48 sorting sidings and ten departure tracks. Down traffic was handled from 17th June 1963 by ten reception sidings, 37 sorting sidings and ten departure tracks. Hump shunting was employed. Between the two sections were a couple of control towers, accommodation for the diesel shunters which worked the yard, and sidings for main line locomotives awaiting their trains. A new signal box was built close to the bridge carrying the Waverley route over the former Caledonian tracks and clusters of floodlights were placed on fifteen 150ft high pylons. The yard was designed to handle 39,000 wagons a week.

Several new or upgraded lines were provided to smooth the approaches to the Kingmoor complex, most of them opening in 1963. A double track connection left the southern end of the Waverley route at Stainton Junction and fed the Carlisle end of the yard. From it sprang up and down goods loops which ran round the eastern and western edges of the site respectively. These formed avoiding lines for through traffic and converged again near the site of Rockcliffe station. The down track then ran alongside the main line as far as Floriston, whilst the up track passed over the former Caledonian route by means of a reinforced concrete flyover and continued its separate course as far as Mossband Junction just south of Gretna.

Efficient handling of traffic to and from the Waverley route posed the greatest difficulties, mainly because the former North British line crossed the West Coast tracks at a higher level immediately south of Kingmoor New Yard. The solution did credit to the planners. Up traffic (from Edinburgh) utilised the revamped Longtown - Gretna branch, which had lost its passenger trains way back in 1915 and was truncated at the Longtown end on 18th July 1960. In this form its sole function was to serve the extensive Naval Ordnance depots and explosives stores, on bleak open ground east of Mossband. The connection to Longtown was reinstated and a new south-facing spur near Gretna providing a link with the up goods line at Mossband Junction. Down traffic (to Edinburgh) was first drawn south along a purpose-built reversing spur which terminated near Stainton Junction. The locomotive then changed ends and hauled its train on to the Waverley route via a connecting line.

Kingmoor New Yard was completed just prior to the publication of 'The Reshaping of British Railways', Dr. Beeching's infamous report. Although this resulted in the closure of hundreds of goods depots throughout the country and many in the Carlisle area, it had little effect on the New Yard at first. In fact there was actually an increase in business at Carlisle - by 1965 over 29,000 wagons a week were being processed at Kingmoor. The vast bulk of these were in transit between yards some distance apart, local traffic being largely concentrated on Dentonholme. Meanwhile, rural sidings and transit sheds together with the once ubiquitous 'pick-up' goods were fading into history. Even within a 25 mile radius of

Top. All manner of engines were used on inter-yard transfers in Carlisle. Fowler 2-6-4T No.42313 of Kingmoor shed heads trip K44 past Caldew Junction in bright sunshine on 30th August 1961. The long string of wagons bound for Upperby carried steel tubes, cement and oil amongst other commodities. Approach tracks to Viaduct yard veer away to the right and the former Caledonian main line is in the background. Photograph Alec Swain.

Middle. In bright autumn sunshine 9F 2-10-0 No.92069 crosses Etterby viaduct with a loaded northbound coal train on 28th October 1967. Photograph W.A.C. Smith.

Left. Together with the Cowans Sheldon crane works and the railways themselves, Carr's biscuit factory provided much of the industrial employment in Carlisle. The company operated this immaculate 0-4-0 Fireless loco, DESPATCH, built by Andrew Barclay in 1915. It is seen on 2nd July 1966. Photograph J.F. Ward.

K1 2-6-0 No.62030 of Blaydon shed heads east through Haltwhistle with a train of mineral empties from London Road yard on 12th April 1952. Photograph J.W. Armstrong Trust.

Carlisle, closures came thick and fast, as the following examples show:
Bulgill (M&C), Leegate (M&C), Plumpton (LNW): 2nd March 1964; Armathwaite (Mid), Cummertrees (G&SW), Eastriggs (G&SW), Kirkpatrick (Cal), Kirtlebridge (Cal), Racks (G&SW), Ruthwell (G&SW): 6th April 1964; Abbey Town (NB), Burgh (NB); Kirkbride (NB), Silloth (NB): 1st June 1964; Langwathby (Mid), Little Saldkeld (Mid), Shap (LNW), Southwaite (LNW): 6th July 1964; Culgaith (Mid), Lyneside (NB): 5th October 1964; Lazonby & Kirkoswald (Mid): 2nd November 1964.

The pace slowed over the next three years, but there were still a dozen goods depot closures around Carlisle, including facilities at some fair-sized places: Heads Nook (NE): 5th April 1965; Brampton Junction (NE): 5th July 1965; Alston (NE): 6th September 1965; Brayton (M&C): 27th September 1965; Lockerbie (Cal): 22nd November 1965; Harker (NB): 27th December 1965; Dumfries St. Mary's (Cal): 17th October 1966; Riddings Junction (NB): 2nd January 1967; Aspatria (M&C): 30th January 1967; Gretna Green (G&SW): 3rd April 1967; Langholm (NB) 18th September 1967; Newcastleton (NB): 9th October 1967.

There were just four closures over the following three years: Dalston (M&C): 5th February 1968; Maryport (M&C) 12th August 1968; Longtown (NB): 31st August 1970; Wigton (M&C): 5th October 1970.

By this time the demise of local goods services and the concentration of most other traffic at Kingmoor had changed the Carlisle railway scene for ever. The former LNWR depot at Crown Street closed officially on 1st February 1966, although the track had been lifted by the previous July. Viaduct yard, once an essential part of Caledonian goods operations in the Border City, expired on 2nd August 1965. Petteril Bridge, where Midland freight via the Settle & Carlisle had been handled, became redundant on 1st February 1966. The historic but antiquated North British yard at Canal closed on 31st May 1969, followed by Bog depot (formerly Maryport & Carlisle) and St. Nicholas (LNWR) on 5th October 1970 and 7th October 1970 respectively. This left just Dentonholme for general traffic and London Road as a coal concentration depot.

For the time being, Kingmoor New Yard remained fairly busy, although the six year old spur from Stainton Junction closed in August 1969 and the down side was phased out during 1972. By this time English Electric, BR Sulzer and Brush type 4 diesels (later class 40, 45 and 47 respectively) were hauling freight traffic south of the Border and English Electric type 3s (class 37) worked trains to and from Scotland and Tyneside.

BR introduced its Speedlink services for wagonload customers during 1977 and in October 1981 Carlisle was designated a 'Main Yard'. This did not dispel rumours that Kingmoor would close completely by the end of the year, however! Indeed, there was a major rationalisation in January 1982 when half of the up side was taken out of use. Nevertheless, Carlisle was still dealing with up to 26 Speedlink trains on weekdays in 1985, the yard seeing all but six of them between 6.00pm and 6.00am. Services included Mossend - Willesden, Warrington - Bathgate, Stranraer - Tyne Yard, Tees Yard - Stranraer and Severn Tunnel Junction - Mossend.

Shortly afterwards, with rumblings of privatisation and government policy preventing cross-subsidy of BR's freight operations, the loss-making Speedlink operation was wound up and yet more traffic was forced to use the roads. This was the death blow to Kingmoor and by the early 1990s hardly anything remained of the massive complex.

Meanwhile, the rest of Carlisle's once comprehensive goods system was being dismantled. In 1978 most sidings at Dentonholme were lifted as part of a pro-road philosophy adopted by National Carriers Ltd., who had inherited the depot. During 1979 the avoiding lines had a brief spell of glory when King's Cross - Edinburgh passenger trains were diverted through Hexham and Carstairs via London Road Junction, Bog Junction and Caldew Junction in Carlisle, as a result of the collapse of Penmanshiel tunnel north of Berwick on Tweed. Five years later the avoiding lines expired in a spectacular manner..... On 1st May 1984 a northbound freightliner train split as it approached Carlisle. The rear portion slowed, then became a runaway which the signalling staff were able to divert on to the goods loop. It careered along out of control until derailing just before the Caldew bridge north of Rome Street Junction. The wagons jacknifed and smashed into the first two spans, plunging part of the structure into the river along with most of the containers. Although the line from Rome Street Junction to Caldew Junction was rendered unusable by the accident, it was not closed officially until December 1985 - well over a year after the damaged section of the bridge was dismantled! On 4th September 1986 Citadel was resignalled to provide reversible goods lines through the station, thus more or less turning the clock back to the 1860s.

A fragment of the Goods Traffic Committee lines survived in the form of a spur from Bog Junction to the Metal Box works at Dentonholme, which lasted until August 1989. Far more significant was the closure of the branch to Cowan Sheldon's factory near London Road. In the guise of Clarke Chapman, the firm had been supplying BR with new breakdown cranes as recently as 1979. When rail traffic ceased in February 1990 it really was the end of an era.

Above. B1 4-6-0 No.61099 pauses at Longtown on the Waverley route with a fitted freight from Millerhill to Kingmoor New Yard, on 6th April 1963. Photograph W.A.C. Smith.

Below. Looking south from the bridge carrying the main road to West Cumberland, Black 5 No.45295 passes Dentonholme North Junction and heads for Caldew Junction with a lengthy freight on 2nd September 1967. The cleared site of Viaduct yard is on the left, whilst to the right a bridge took the Dentonholme loop across the River Caldew. Dentonholme Goods box beyond the signal post controlled movement in the yard. Photograph W.A.C. Smith.

Above. The ancient and gloomy interior of Canal shed during the mid-1950s with two ex-North British residents - J36 0-6-0 No.65216 BYNG and N15 0-6-2T No.69174. Photograph Neville Stead Collection.

Below. Four 4-4-2Ts of London Tilbury & Southend Railway design were sent from Essex to Dundee Tay Bridge in 1950, presumably as replacements for C15s and C16s, only to receive a frosty welcome. In fact they were sent back to England and got as far as Carlisle, to languish for years thereafter in a siding at Durranhill shed, before being cut up. Nos. 41972, 41974 and 41973 are nearest the camera. Photograph Neville Stead Collection.

Chapter 11
ENGINE SHEDS

As outlined in previous chapters, Carlisle was the meeting place of seven independent companies, a point where many expresses took on a fresh engine, and a major centre for the exchange of freight traffic. It is therefore hardly surprising that there was a proliferation of engine sheds in the Border City. There were up to twenty of them at one time or another, in all shapes and sizes and with a very mixed history. Duties were as diverse as main line runs to London and trip workings between local goods yards, and the range of engines reflected these multifarious requirements. Of the score or so of sheds, less than half existed in 'historic times' (since the 1870s, say) and many are obscure, little known sites from the confused dark ages of our railways. What follows can only be an outline, and there is doubtless more 'archaeological' material yet to be unearthed - the latest, and probably most exhaustive treatment of this convoluted subject, by Roger Griffiths, is to be found in Link, the journal of the Engine Shed Society.

The North Eastern Railway's shed was at London Road, about three quarters of a mile east of Citadel. In later years its allocation included various 4-4-0 and 0-6-0 tender engines for working passenger and goods trains across the Tyne Gap to Newcastle as well as a few small tanks such as the BTP 0-4-4s for local passenger services to Haltwhistle and Brampton. It survived for a while after Grouping, finally closing in 1933. The remaining locomotives were transferred to the ex-North British Canal shed which then became responsible for the turns to and from Newcastle not covered by Gateshead. However, the yard was used as a servicing point for NER locos until the early 1960s. Typically amongst the Carlisle sheds, London Road had earlier, murky beginnings - the Newcastle & Carlisle had arrived in 1836 to its London Road terminus and the first shed on the site had been a two road affair. This burned down and the latter day shed, a pair of roundhouses with a further turntable outside, grew up from the 1860s.

Maryport & Carlisle engines had two homes in the city. Bog (or Bogfield) shed stood near the junction with the

CARLISLE CATHEDRAL

Coronation Pacifics Nos 46237 CITY OF BRISTOL (in green livery) and 46251 CITY OF NOTTINGHAM (in red) pose at Upperby shed yard on 12th July 1964. Their premature withdrawal from service came just two months later. Photograph W.A.C. Smith.

The Maryport & Carlisle shed at Currock in pre-grouping days. Note the little projections at the eaves, a familiar feature of the company's buildings. Very neat 2-4-0 No.8 and 0-4-2 No.4 were built at Maryport works in 1876 and 1879 respectively. They were renumbered 10006 and 10010 by the LMS, but the 2-4-0 expired in 1925 and the 0-4-2 was scrapped in 1928. Photograph F.W. Shuttleworth Collection.

Newcastle & Carlisle's Canal branch just over a quarter of a mile from Citadel and opened in the mid-1840s. In January 1876 it was replaced by larger premises at Currock, 1/4 mile further south nearer Currock Junction. This move was largely brought about by the remodelling of the southern approaches to Citadel. Currock shared passenger and goods duties with the shed at Maryport for nearly half a century, but it closed in 1923 shortly after Grouping. At first, ex-Maryport & Carlisle engines went to the nearby G&SW depot, but that was doomed too and they ended their working lives at Upperby.

Upperby was in operation for longer than any other Carlisle shed. It stood on the eastern side of the West Coast main line just over 3/4 mile south of Citadel and the first buildings were established by the Lancaster & Carlisle in 1846. This shed (or sheds) lay north of the Upperby we know, in the district of 'Botchergate'. 'Upperby' proper, moulded from various works buildings, had come into use by the mid-1870s and was a grand 'steam shed' of typically lofty LNW appearance. Throughout its time, the finest main line engines graced the yard. This was still the case under LMS and BR ownership, with the shed boasting a sizeable allocation of Duchess Pacifics. A modern, circular roundhouse in concrete and glass was built on the site by BR in 1948 but plans to modernise the yard were not properly seen through. Upperby closed to steam on 31st December 1966 but was not demolished for another ten years.

For a quarter of a century, Caledonian engines were serviced at West Walls shed on the east side of the main line, a quarter of a mile or so north of Citadel. Unfortunately, this cramped site was a matter of yards from the Dean of Carlisle's study window (it is famously recorded) and smoke from locomotives gave rise to endless acrimonious correspondence with the Caledonian board. The matter was resolved in 1873 when Kingmoor shed was built in open country 1 1/2 miles further north, again on the east side of the tracks. Opening first as a cavernous wooden building (the place was known then as 'Etterby') in 1876-77, it was replaced by a modern brick structure during the Great War. This was the shed we know as 'Kingmoor', by this time a vast establishment serving the Scottish section of the West Coast main. Kingmoor closed on 31st December 1967.

From 1850 G&SW locomotives used the Caledonian shed at West Walls, but the arch-rivalry between these two companies resulted in a somewhat strained co-habitation. When Kingmoor (or 'Etterby') opened the Sou'West was offered space there, but decided to seek refuge with the Midland, its new English ally. G&SW engines used part of the Durranhill site (which they tended to call Petteril) from April 1875. Finally, in 1894, independent facilities were opened at Currock on the east side of the Maryport & Carlisle loop from Currock Junction, about a mile from Citadel. This shed was only a couple of hundred yards from the smaller company's depot and running powers were granted over Maryport tracks. Currock ex-G&SW was closed by the LMS in 1924 and most main line 4-4-0s and 4-6-0s went to Kingmoor. This caused ill-feeling bordering on aggression among Sou'West men, who regarded the LMS as the 'Caley in maroon'! The shed survived as a wagon repair shop.

Modest locomotive facilities for the Silloth line existed near its southern terminus from the mid-1850s, but Canal

Durranhill, a substantial square 'roundhouse' typical of the Midland Railway, in 1935. The row of 0-6-0s on the right, headed by 2F No.3084, looks fairly moribund, but the 4-4-0 and 'Crab' Moguls are clearly ready for work. Photograph Heyday Publishing Company.

shed proper dated from the opening of the Waverley route in 1862. Although not quite as far out as Kingmoor, the North British shed was very much on the edge of the city and 1½ miles from Citadel. It occupied a strip of land between the Silloth branch and the River Eden immediately after the divergence of the Waverley route. From the early years Canal worked local passenger and goods trains to Silloth, Langholm and Hawick as well as through services to Edinburgh, a role which continued for almost a century. However, the shed really came into its element when the Settle & Carlisle opened in 1876. Top-link engines were maintained there for taking over Anglo-Scottish expresses and from the late 1920s to the advent of diesels these were Gresley A3 Pacifics. Canal closed on 17th June 1963 and the remaining allocation was transferred to Kingmoor.

A roundhouse in best Midland tradition opened at Durranhill in time for the start of goods traffic over the Settle & Carlisle during 1875. It stood a mile east of Petteril Bridge Junction and almost 1½ miles from Citadel. For nearly fifty years it was the exclusive domicile of the 0-6-0s, 2-4-0s and 4-4-0s which pounded the high fells. Along with the Settle & Carlisle itself, Durranhill became the poor relation of the West Coast operation, which of course included Upperby shed. Nevertheless, some new 'Crab' 2-6-0s were sent to the erstwhile Midland shed to satisfy the needs of the former G&SW route. Closure came on 15th February 1936, but the sheer volume of wartime traffic led to its necessarily secret reopening during the early 1940s. It was intended for 'turnback' engines and Upperby sent cleaners over on every shift to work a crude coaling 'conveyer' machine. When hostilities ceased there was sufficient goods work on the Settle & Carlisle to keep Durranhill open, albeit on a fairly low-key basis. In addition to 4F 0-6-0s, 'Crabs' and Black 5 4-6-0s for freight duties, there was even the odd Jubilee for passenger services to Leeds. Final closure came in November 1959. When the last loyal incumbent eased into the bosom of Upperby shed, the spirits of the LNWR board no doubt smiled.

CANAL, UPPERBY AND KINGMOOR

As noted above, Carlisle's three principal sheds survived into the 1960s. Under the custodianship of British Railways they remained busy places and provided a great deal of local employment. By the very nature of their work, they were grimy and unattractive to casual observers; as far as enthusiasts were concerned they were Mecca. The legacy of the Victorian railway companies was still present during the 1950s in the form of several pre-grouping classes. The might of LMS and LNER motive power was also there, resting in sheds barely two miles apart before backing on to their respective expresses. Where else did locally-based Gresley A3s and Stanier Coronations rub shoulders every day at the same station?

CANAL (68E) Allocation Summer 1955 (Total 53)

Gresley A3 4-6-2 (Ex-LNER):
60068 SIR VISTO, 60079 BAYARDO, 60093 CORONACH, 60095 FLAMINGO

Thompson B1 4-6-0 (LNER designed):
61064, 61217, 61219, 61222, 61239, 61290

Gresley K3 2-6-0 (ex-LNER):
61851, 61854, 61858, 61882, 61898, 61916, 61936, 61937

Gresley D49 4-4-0 (ex-LNER):
62732 DUMFRIES-SHIRE, 62734 CUMBERLAND

Reid J35 0-6-0 (ex-North British):
64478, 64499, 64526

Gresley J39 0-6-0 (Ex-LNER):
64727, 64733, 64875, 64877, 64880, 64884, 64888, 64892, 64895, 64899, 64912, 64930, 64932, 64948, 64964

Holmes J36 0-6-0 (Ex-North British):
65216 BYNG, 65293, 65304, 65312, 65321

Reid C15 4-4-2T (Ex-North British):
67458, 67481

Reid N15 0-6-2T (Ex-North British):
69139, 69155, 69174, 69215

Ivatt 4MT 2-6-0 (LMS designed):
43139

Fairburn/English Electric 0-6-0 Diesel Shunter (ex-LMS): 12084, 12085, 12086

CANAL DUTIES

The four A3s were, of course, primarily intended for the Waverley route expresses and received a great deal of pampering; indeed, they gained quite a reputation for their immaculate condition. Canal's Gresley Pacifics enjoyed long tenancies, FLAMINGO being shedded there for almost the whole of its 33 years. Stopping passenger trains to Edinburgh and Newcastle had been hauled by Scotts and Shires until the early 1950s, but by 1955 B1s had more or less taken over despite the lingering presence of a couple of D49s. Express freights to Tyneside and over the Waverley route were monopolised by the K3s, although a B1 occasionally got a look in.

Local goods and transfer trips were the preserve of the 0-6-0s, although the J39s also worked Silloth and Langholm branch passenger services. The N15s shunted Canal yard and the C15s were, at least nominally, employed as Collier Lane carriage sidings pilots. A real oddity was the solitary Ivatt mogul. It was a regular performer on the morning and evening workers' trains to Parkhouse Halt serving the nearby RAF Maintenance Unit. After transfer to Kingmoor on closure of Canal shed, it had the dubious distinction of working the last Silloth passenger train. The former North British depot experienced a decline from 1955; Newcastle-based diesel multiple units were destined to take over Carlisle workings and the authorities decided to employ Edinburgh St Margarets engines on out and home turns for most Waverley route trains.

UPPERBY DUTIES

Along with Camden, Crewe and Polmadie, Upperby had the cream of West Coast motive power. The Princess Coronations were, of course, normally reserved for the

Unrebuilt Patriot 4-6-0 No.45503 THE ROYAL LEICESTERSHIRE REGIMENT on the outside turntable at Upperby, 11th August 1956. Photograph W.A.C. Smith.

principal expresses to Euston, although they sometimes appeared on less glamorous duties. The Patriots, Jubilees and Scots also hauled main line passenger trains, including those to Birmingham, Manchester and Liverpool, as well as parcels traffic and express freights over the former LNWR route. Apparently the Jubilees were very popular at Upperby as they could be worked hard uphill - a real asset on the routes south. All manner of passenger and goods work was undertaken by the versatile Black 5s.

The 4Fs could usually be found on local goods duties and the 3F 'Jinty' 0-6-0Ts shunted the various yards on the south side of Carlisle, as well as working transfer trips. They also acted as south end station pilots. West Cumberland and Keswick trains were the preserve of the 2Ps, but around this time Upperby also had several 2-6-4Ts for such duties. Even the former LNWR 0-6-0s had the occasional outing to Penrith and Keswick when nothing else was available for hauling passenger trains, but generally they pottered around on local goods traffic.

The great Ramsbottom hipped-roof 'steam shed' that was Upperby was in tumble-down condition and due for rebuilding well before the outbreak of the Second World War, when almost the only remaining roof portion was that over the arrangements board! It was no surprise that BR rebuilt the place as a matter of urgency. There was always a tremendous amount of trip work through Carlisle and in World War Two the whole system was strained to breaking - the carriage shed yard at Upperby would fill with locos, often from every shed in the city. They were 'returned' dead in runs of half a dozen or more, to great consternation at the 'home' shed.

Ivatt 2MT 2-6-0s arrived for the Keswick locals in the early 1950s, whilst the odd 4MT 2-6-0 appeared some years later. During the last years of steam traction a few Stanier 2-8-0s were housed at Upperby and there was also super-power in the form of 9F 2-10-0s. As new diesels were concentrated at Kingmoor in the late 1960s, the former LNWR depot tended to become a refuge for steam locomotives in store, most of which never worked again. Closure came at the end of December 1967, but diesel multiple units for Keswick and West Cumberland services continued to stable there.

KINGMOOR DUTIES

Kingmoor passenger links, despite the allocation of Clans, Jubilees and Black 5s, more often than not involved the re-manning of through workings from other depots, hence the lack of large Pacifics until the run-down of steam in the early 1960s. The shed did, however, provide power for the Stranraer boat trains, Sou'West locals, the 'Parly' (all stations to Carstairs), parcels trains, piloting and special workings. Thus, on the last Monday in September for example, a procession of Black 5s could be seen heading north with Glasgow Autumn Holiday excursions returning from Blackpool. But the large allocation of Stanier 5MTs was mainly intended for the numerous express freights dispatched, often overnight, from the various yards in the city. The Crabs also took turns on these workings.

As well as literally so, Kingmoor was long a 'border' shed in the politicking (in the sense of attending to Scottish sensibilities) that shaped the LMS and the

UPPERBY (12A) Allocation Winter 1950 (Total 88)

Johnson/Fowler 2P 4-4-0 (ex-Midland):
40356, 40448

Fowler 2P 4-4-0 (ex-LMS):
40652, 40699

Fowler 4F 0-6-0 (ex-LMS):
44081, 44121, 44346, 44390

Stanier 5MT 4-6-0 (ex-LMS):
44869, 44871, 44876, 44936, 44939, 45065, 45106, 45128, 45139, 45184, 45197, 45230, 45244, 45246, 45258, 45293, 45295, 45296, 45299, 45311, 45323, 45345, 45348, 45351, 45368, 45371, 45388, 45409, 45412, 45414, 45416, 45439, 45445, 45451, 45494

Fowler 6P 'Patriot' 4-6-0 (ex-LMS):
45505 THE ROYAL ARMY ORDNANCE CORPS, 45517, 45518 BRADSHAW, 45541, 45542, 45549, 45550, 45551

Fowler/Ivatt 7P rebuilt 'Patriot' 4-6-0 (ex-LMS):
45512 BUNSEN, 45526 MORECAMBE AND HEYSHAM

Stanier 6P 'Jubilee' 4-6-0 (ex-LMS):
45552 SILVER JUBILEE, 45555 QUEBEC, 45578 UNITED PROVINCES, 45595 SOUTHERN RHODESIA, 45624 ST HELENA, 45630 SWAZILAND, 45677 BEATTY, 45687 NEPTUNE, 45718 DREADNOUGHT, 45722 DEFENCE

Fowler/Stanier 7P rebuilt 'Royal Scot' 4-6-0 (ex-LMS):
46136 THE BORDER REGIMENT, 46147 THE NORTHAMPTONSHIRE REGIMENT

Stanier 8P 'Princess Coronation' 4-6-2 (ex-LMS):
46226 DUCHESS OF NORFOLK, 46228 DUCHESS OF RUTLAND, 46238 CITY OF CARLISLE, 46251 CITY OF NOTTINGHAM, 46253 CITY OF ST ALBANS, 46254 CITY OF STOKE-ON-TRENT, 46255 CITY OF HEREFORD

Johnson/Hughes 3F 0-6-0T (ex-LMS):
47295, 47326, 47327, 47340, 47377, 47391, 47403, 47408, 47415, 47556, 47614, 47618, 47664, 47666

Webb 2F 'Cauliflower' 0-6-0 (ex-LNWR):
58376, 58419

Rebuilt Royal Scot No.46140 THE KING'S ROYAL RIFLE CORPS under the coaling plant at Upperby on 8th May 1965. Photograph W.A.C. Smith

KINGMOOR (68A) Allocation Summer 1955 (Total 143)

Fowler 2P 4-4-0 (ex-LMS):
40602, 40613, 40615, 40651

Hughes/Fowler 5MT 2-6-0 (ex-LMS):
42720, 42748, 42751, 42752, 42757, 42831, 42832, 42833, 42834, 42835, 42836, 42837, 42875, 42876, 42877, 42881, 42882, 42883, 42884, 42899, 42905, 42906, 42907

Johnson 3F 0-6-0 (ex-Midland):
43241, 43301, 43351, 43514, 43622, 43636, 43678

Fowler 4F 0-6-0 (ex-Midland):
43868, 43902, 43922, 43973, 44008, 44009, 44016

Fowler 4F 0-6-0 (ex-LMS):
44181, 44183, 44189, 44324, 44326

Stanier 5MT 4-6-0 (ex-LMS):
44668, 44669, 44670, 44671, 44672, 44673, 44674, 44675, 44676, 44725, 44726, 44727, 44790, 44792, 44795, 44877, 44878, 44882, 44883, 44884, 44886, 44898, 44899, 44900, 44901, 44902, 44903, 44993, 45012, 45013, 45018, 45081, 45082, 45083, 45100, 45112, 45118, 45120, 45122, 45126, 45138, 45163, 45281, 45330, 45334, 45363, 45364, 45455, 45466, 45481, 45491

Stanier 6P 'Jubilee' 4-6-0 (ex-LMS):
45640 FROBISHER, 45657 TYRWHITT, 45679 ARMADA, 45691 ORION, 45696 ARETHUSA, 45697 ACHILLES, 45704 LEVIATHAN, 45713 RENOWN, 45714 REVENGE, 45715 INVINCIBLE, 45716 SWIFTSURE, 45718 DREADNOUGHT, 45724 WARSPITE, 45728 DEFIANCE, 45729 FURIOUS, 45730 OCEAN, 45731 PERSEVERANCE, 45732 SANSPAREIL

Stanier 8F 2-8-0 (ex-LMS):
48321, 48464, 48472, 48536, 48612, 48708, 48756, 48758

McIntosh 3F 0-6-0T (ex-Caledonian):
56231, 56235, 56316, 56317, 56332, 56333, 56340, 56355, 56373, 56374

Standard 6MT 4-6-2:
72005 CLAN MACGREGOR, 72006 CLAN MACKENZIE, 72007 CLAN MACKINTOSH, 72008 CLAN MACLEOD, 72009 CLAN STEWART

Riddles WD 'Austerity' 8F 2-8-0 (ex-Ministry of Supply):
90170, 90464

Riddles WD 'Austerity' 8F 2-10-0 (ex-Ministry of Supply):
90763

Fairburn/English Electric 0-6-0 Diesel Shunter (ex-LMS):
12079, 12080

Scottish Region. To some extent it was a law unto itself - in the War for instance Euston issued various decrees, cheerfully ignored.

Kingmoor's 2-8-0s were usually employed on loose-coupled mineral trains, Standard 9F 2-10-0s appearing for such duties in the last years of steam. Local trip workings were in the hands of the 0-6-0s and the instructions for a typical turn in LMS days was as follows: Lockerbie 18in x 26in engine. Kingmoor shed 9.25am. Train Viaduct Yard to Lockerbie and back. Places goods traffic in shed at Lockerbie and works empty milk vans from that station for Kirtlebridge, Kirkpatrick and Gretna. On Saturdays places milk truck for Newcastle in position for attaching by 10.25am Passenger ex-Glasgow Central. Shunting at Rockcliffe, Floriston, Quintinshill and Castlemilk was included and the loco arrived back at Kingmoor at 4.43pm.

Transfer trips between the various yards were worked by the moguls and 0-6-0s, although the appearance of 2-8-0s and even large passenger engines (the latter usually in run-down condition and awaiting works attention) was not uncommon. Shunting turns at Kingmoor, Viaduct and Dentonholme yards were covered by 0-6-0Ts. Such duties are summed up by this example: Viaduct Yard. Turn 112. Locomotive men book on duty at 3.10pm.

Top right. Pickersgill 0-6-0 No.57653 and LMS 0-6-0T No.47354 simmer at Kingmoor on 15th June 1958. Photograph W.A.C. Smith.

Right. Work-stained 9F No.92069, 8F No.48679 and a Black 5 darken the sky at Kingmoor shed on 26th September 1966. Photograph W.A.C. Smith.

Engine from sheds 3.55pm. Relieve Turn 105 for locomotive duties. Work 6.50pm Viaduct Yard to Kingmoor. Thereafter to Viaduct Yard and shunt there 8.45pm to 10.45pm. Thence to sheds.

Kingmoor provided the Citadel north end station pilot and this was normally drawn from the ranks of the 0-6-0Ts, but the former CR engines were replaced by LM 3F tanks in the late 1950s.

After closure of Canal in 1963 the shed serviced Edinburgh A3s and V2s which had worked hard on heavy freights over the Waverley route. Kingmoor now began to accumulate Britannias, 8Fs and 9Fs, the 2-10-0s proving both highly capable and very popular. When Kingmoor closed at the end of 1967 its diesels were transferred to a specially-built depot on the west side of the main line. The allocation there consisted principally of shunters but main line locomotives were fuelled and cleaned until electrification diminished even this role. Now, other than a few overgrown patches of wasteland, where the wind hisses through grass and shrubs, and the feet of those paying homage turn up an occasional brick or piece of concrete, little remains of the greatest concentration of main line sheds seen in this country.

Above. The south end of Kingmoor on 30th April 1966 with 9F No.92076, Britannia No.70046 ANZAC and Black 5 No.44903 on the right. Another Britannia, No.70009 ALFRED THE GREAT is on the left. All the locomotives were based at Kingmoor. Photograph J.F. Ward Collection.

Below. Coronation Pacific No.46255 CITY OF HEREFORD in immaculate external condition takes water at Kingmoor shed prior to working the SLS 'Coronation Pacific Pennine Summits' railtour over Ais Gill on 12th July 1964. Photograph W.A.C. Smith.

Chapter 12
CITADEL 150

Although this book follows the general pattern of others in the Irwell Press *Illustrated History* series, it was written specifically for the 150th anniversary of Citadel station. Consequently, a chapter has been included on the Carlisle railway scene in 1997. As outlined in previous chapters, the city can boast a rich history of company rivalry, passenger services, goods workings and motive power - reasons enough for a celebration. However, present-day operations contain plenty of interest and Citadel itself remains a very fine station. Elsewhere in the city there are many tangible reminders of the great days and these are well worth seeking out.

Carlisle still has the appearance of a busy market town rather than a provincial city and although there are plenty of fine buildings in the centre, they are on a relatively modest scale. Even the castle and cathedral hardly tower above their surroundings. Indeed, it is remarkable how Dixon's 1836 cotton mill remains a dominant feature of Carlisle. The city is a service centre for a huge area of Border country, and The Lanes shopping complex, built on the site of sub-standard Victorian and Georgian houses, is one of the best in England.

Compared with some current main line stations, Citadel has weathered the rationalisation and modernisation process of recent years extremely well. Apart from the scissors crossings, the track layout is more or less the same as it was in the 1950s (and for that matter the 1880s). Even the west side carriage sidings have found alternative uses. All eight platforms remain, with West Cumberland and Newcastle services using their dedicated bays in time-honoured fashion. The surviving section of overall roof retains its 1881 appearance, apart from the end screens of course. However, the 1957 umbrella canopies are decaying in places.

The island platform, in particular, has some exquisite details worth seeking out. Some of the original etched glass in the buffet windows remains, whilst the magnificent first floor bay window of former No.4A signal box still appears to supervise the main through roads. The ramp from Victoria Viaduct continues to provide access to the station and the ornate bridge itself is virtually unchanged. An incidental bonus is that Citadel's broad, gently-humped lattice footbridge provides an excellent vantage point for steam engines on the not infrequent specials, reviving memories of the 1960s and beyond.

Modernisation of the entrance hall was completed in 1986. There is a bookstall opposite the ticket windows and a fairly intimate atmosphere prevails; in fact it is amazing how all the pre-grouping booking office facilities were crammed into this space. Tite's wonderful 1850 frontage has altered hardly at all, and would be instantly recognisable to early Victorian travellers. The three coats of arms have been picked out in red, white, blue and gold, but there are still two blank shields, seemingly awaiting acknowledgement of the Newcastle & Carlisle and Maryport & Carlisle presence.

Back inside the station, there is still a fair variety of traffic to be seen. Furthermore, the number of liveries introduced over the last decade or so have made Citadel slightly reminiscent of pre-grouping days. This applies particularly to the Sprinters and Pacers which provide the local services. Regional Railways units in standard two-tone blue and grey

The southern approach to Citadel, in brilliant autumn sunshine on 16th September 1996. No.90008 THE BIRMINGHAM ROYAL BALLET approaches platform 3 with the down 'Royal Scot' which left London Euston for Glasgow Central at 10.40. To the left, Vasey's store occupies the site of the former LNWR Crown Street goods depot. Photograph W.A.C. Smith.

An Illustrated History of Carlisle's Railways

No. 86260 DRIVER WALLACE OAKES GC runs into platform 4 with the 12.30 from Glasgow Central to Poole on 16th September 1996. Victoria Viaduct and the fine red sandstone buildings at the north end of Citadel station, erected well over a century ago, provide links with pre-grouping days. Photograph W.A.C. Smith.

mingle with trains from Newcastle in yellow and white, together with those from Glasgow in Strathclyde orange and black. Vehicles in North West red and grey and West Yorkshire red and cream come in over the Cumbrian coast and Settle & Carlisle routes respectively. New liveries will no doubt appear as various franchise holders decide on their corporate styles. The familiar and somewhat sedate InterCity colours are about to give way to something more striking as Richard Branson's Virgin Cross Country and West Coast operations begin to establish their identity. Bright red, just chosen for the

The north end of Citadel on 16th September 1996, little changed from the late 1950s, apart from overhead wires and, of course, the motive power. 86206 CITY OF STOKE ON TRENT (echoes of Stanier Pacifics here!) leaves platform 3 with the 05.54 from Bournemouth to Edinburgh. Photograph W.A.C. Smith.

Citadel's robust east side wall, despite having relinquished its role as a support for the overall roof many years ago, still formed a rather fine backdrop to the essential clutter of an electrified railway, on 16th September 1996. With power car No.43197 leading, an InterCity 125 forming 'The Devon Scot' (09.10 Aberdeen - Plymouth) leaves platform 4 as 37154 and 37240 wait on one of the centre roads with a track maintenance train. Photograph W.A.C. Smith.

former at the time of writing, has been seen at Carlisle for some time on Rail Express Systems and Royal Mail carriages. On the freight side, Wisconsin Central's EW&S deep red and cream livery is becoming increasingly common on locomotives passing through Citadel. An 08 shunter is employed at Carlisle, although in 1997 this languished in faded and now historic Railfreight grey.

Carlisle is a compact city and most former railway sites can be explored on foot within a few hours. For the less energetic, there are frequent Stagecoach bus services to the suburbs. Although a de-

No. 47489 CREWE DIESEL DEPOT at platform 4 with an up parcels train, on 16th September 1996. Photograph W.A.C. Smith.

'The Tyne Enterprise', 10.00 Stranraer Harbour to Newcastle, formed by Sprinter 156431 leaves platform 4 on 16th September 1996 as Pacer 142054 waits at No.2 bay with the 13.46 for Whitehaven. The trains will cover the two lines which arrived at Carlisle before Citadel was built. Photograph W.A.C. Smith.

gree of nostalgia for the days of steam and abundant traffic is bound to arise, exploring the city's railway heritage is far from depressing. Enough remains to allow the mind to recreate scenes portrayed earlier in this book.

Just beyond the Infirmary and next to an estate of modern houses off Newtown Road, a rough track leads down to the site of Canal shed. Numerous drivers and firemen no doubt walked along this lane prior to taking over an A3, easing it into Citadel and backing on to an Edinburgh express. The course of the Silloth branch is merely a ditch nowadays, but a stone viaduct where the Waverley route crossed the River Eden is an impressive survivor. Wasteland of a rural nature has replaced the actual depot. Looking at the scene today, it is astonishing how a main line shed managed to function in such a constricted area.

An unofficial but well-trod path follows the former railway round the back of the hospital to the site of Canal yard and the exchange sidings. This particular locality is being developed as an industrial estate. One of the red sandstone abutments where the Canal branch crossed Newtown Road remains, but the formation either side of it has vanished.

A little further towards the city centre, Carr's biscuit factory emanates sweet aromas and the State Brewery stands proudly alongside the River Caldew, albeit in the form of student flats. On the right, a new service road slips down to the site of Viaduct yard. The erstwhile shunting neck, once the source of so much congestion, is occupied by a tile warehouse and the Cumbria Indoor Bowls Club. The rest of the former Caledonian depot has been taken over by two car showrooms and their associated parking lots.

Fortunately, but no doubt unintentionally, these developments provide enthusiasts with a previously inaccessible view of the main line north of Citadel. The tracks are at eye level, just beyond a low stone wall, and photographic opportunities are good. Beyond the metals, the cathedral peeps above a succession of dignified red sandstone buildings belonging to the church authorities. The Dean's study window is still there and it is easy to see why he was incensed by the smoke and noise from West Walls shed and yard, the site of which remains.

On the far side of the erstwhile shunting neck, a new path called the Caldew Riverside Trail follows the course of the former Goods Committee lines. There is little evidence of the bridge where the Dentonholme loop crossed the Caldew, but the site of the yard itself is easily identified by a series of small industrial units on the far side of the river. The footpath soon spans rushing water from the slopes of Skiddaw on hefty girders erected for the avoiding line. To the right, a tall timber pole of railway origin carries floodlights for illuminating a lorry yard, whilst the former G&SW goods shed is now a road transport depot. Dixon's mighty textile mill oversees this scene.

The Riverside Trail ends just short of the broken bridge which bears silent witness to the catastrophic freightliner derailment of 1984. Ironically, one of the gantries for the overhead wires still springs from the remaining side girders. A walk through the back streets of Dentonholme reveals numerous small terraced houses where many of Carlisle's railwaymen once lived. In nearby Denton Street, two fine bridge abutments dating from the late 1830s are another reminder of the Newcastle & Carlisle's Canal branch. The route back to Citadel crosses Nelson Bridge, which incorporates plaques detailing its history - Carlisle seems to have been fond of celebrating bridges in this manner, as can be seen elsewhere in the city.

A mile or so away on the other side of Carlisle, the site of the Midland goods yard at Petteril Bridge is occupied by an engineering factory, but a single storey brick building survives near London Road and is used by a builders' merchant. Nearby, Durranhill shed has been cleared and the area fenced off, although a colony of unmistakably Midland housing remains. At present, the former North Eastern complex at London Road retains several substantial buildings in the company's late Victorian style. Some are derelict, but others have been adapted for non-railway uses, the motor trade inevitably being one of them. The large Cowans Sheldon factory on the other side of London Road has been replaced by a supermarket, but the old tram depot still stands. St. Nicholas Street bridge reveals a view of Citadel's southern approaches and the goods lines, easily recognisably from earlier photographs. Further on, the site of Currock G&SW shed is now occupied by Currock Wagon Repair Depot, currently painting vans in EW&S colours. Nearby South Western Terrace, leading down from Currock Road, has a fine row of company houses - it is almost possible to smell engine smoke here! Currock Road crosses the goods lines on a metal bridge announcing that it was built by P&W MacClellan, Clutha Ironworks, Glasgow 1876.

A detailed map as well as imagination is needed to locate the course of the original Maryport & Carlisle approach to Bog yard. However, a sandstone warehouse which was once part of the depot is clearly visible from the platform ends at Citadel. On the opposite side of the main line, Crown Street yard has succumbed to Vasey's Stylestore. Upperby and Kingmoor are best viewed from the train. The former still has an extensive array of sidings for stabling engineers' wagons and a large LNWR building survives. Kingmoor steam shed has long gone, but the nearby trainmen's hostel has been converted into flats. Sadly, the New Yard is just a straggle of little-used sidings and the power box is derelict.

Perhaps an antidote is needed after viewing all these ghosts of the great days. A journey over any of the six surviving lines out of Carlisle is as interesting as ever and some of the original wayside station buildings remain. For example, there is a glimpse of Lancaster & Carlisle Tudor Gothic at Wreay and Southwaite from a Virgin West Coast express. The continuity of 150 years of railway services to and from Carlisle Citadel is as poignant here as anywhere.

Top. A pair of Class 156 Sprinters bound for Stranraer Harbour, the nearer in orange and black Strathclyde livery, stand at platform 1 on 16th September 1996. The train is 'The Galloway Enterprise' which departed from Newcastle at 12.37. Photograph W.A.C. Smith.

Middle. The Waverley route service today! A MacEwan Leyland coach waits to leave Citadel station forecourt with the 13.55 to Langholm, Hawick, Selkirk and Galashiels on 16th September 1996. The *Borders Town Bus/Rail Link* is operated under contract to local councils, with half a dozen services daily. Photograph W.A.C. Smith.

Right. Having narrowly escaped closure, the Settle & Carlisle line is now being marketed as one of Carlisle's principal tourist attractions. With a fine example of 'Derby Gothic' standing proudly on the down platform, a pair of Class 156 Sprinters forming the 14.27 from Carlisle to Leeds calls at Langwathby on 22nd August 1992. This station was one of those reopened in 1986. The Midland building is now the 'Brief Encounter' restaurant and the 'Friends of the Setttle and Carlisle line' plan to reinstate a waiting shelter on the up platform. Photograph W.A.C. Smith.

Carlisle's purley diesel era - between the end of prolific main line steam and electrification - was fairly brief. It was also quite distinctive. As electrification work proceeded, West Coast AEI class 85 No. 85019 awaits departure from Carlisle on 24 January 1981, with the return portion of a steam-hauled Settle & Carlisle 'Cumbrian Mountain Express' for Crewe and the south. Photograph. Brian Morrison.

And finally.... over the last twenty years Carlisle has become a Mecca for steam enthusiasts again. Fairly frequent workings by preserved locomotives have used the Settle & Carlisle line, although the Newcastle, Sou'West and West Coast routes have recently featured as well. On 2nd October 1993 Stanier Pacific No.46203 PRINCESS MARGARET ROSE stands at platform 4, having arrived with one of the popular 'Cumbrian Mountain Express' specials. Photograph W.A.C. Smith.